Insider's guide to Mexico and Central America | page 1
Introduction
Mexico City
Tijuana and Baja California, Puerto Vallarta, Guadalajara, Acapulco,
Oaxaca, Veracruz, The Yucatán
Guatemala, Costa Rica and Cuba
Holidays, festivals and events

Bare necessities | page 30
Essential words and phrases
Numbers, times, days of the week

Getting around | page 38
Traveling around Latin America: car rental and public transportation

Somewhere to stay | page 48
Finding accommodations: hotels, rentals, campsites

Buying things | page 56
Food, clothes, stamps

Café life | page 68
Getting drinks and snacks

Eating out | page 76
Ordering a meal

Menu reader | page 84
Understanding menus in Latin America

Entertainment and leisure | page 90
Finding events, getting tickets and information

Emergencies | page 98
Doctors, dentists, pharmacies, car breakdown, theft

Language builder | page 108
The basics of Spanish grammar

Answers | page 112
Key to Language works and Try it out

Dictionary | page 114
Full list of Spanish words with
English translations

Sounds Spanish | page 124, inside cover
Simple guide to pronouncing Spanish

INTRODUCTION

Get Around in Mexico and Central America will enable you to pick up the language, travel with confidence and experience the very best the countries of Latin America have to offer. You can use it both *before* a trip, to pick up the basics of the language and to plan your itinerary, and *during* your trip, as a phrasebook and as a source of practical information in all the key travel situations.

Contents
Insider's guide to Mexico An introduction to the country, a guide to the main cities and region-by-region highlights for planning itineraries.
Bare necessities The absolute essentials.
Seven main chapters covering key travel situations from *Getting around* to *Entertainment and leisure*. Each chapter has three main sections: *information* to help you understand the local way of doing things; *Phrasemaker*, a phrasebook of key words and phrases; *Language works/Try it out*, simple dialogues and activities to help you remember the language.
Menu reader A key to menus in Latin America.
Language builder A simple introduction to the grammar.
1000-word dictionary The most important Spanish words you will come across with their English translations.
Sounds Spanish A clear guide to pronouncing the language.

How to use the book
Before you go You can use the *Insider's guide* to get a flavor of the country and plan where you want to go. To pick up the language, the *Phrasemaker* sections give you the key words and phrases; the *Language works* dialogues show the language in action, and *Try it out* offers you a chance to practice for yourself.

During your trip The *Insider's guide* offers tips on the best things to see and do in the main cities. The *Phrasemaker* works as a phrasebook with all the key language to help you get what you want. Within each chapter there is also practical "survival" information to help you get around and understand Mexico and Central America.

Insider's guide to Mexico

Mexico's historical setting

Mexico is the most populous Spanish-speaking nation in the world. Yet before the Hispanic Conquistadores imposed the language in the 16th century, the country was home to some of the world's greatest civilizations. Indeed, the remains of the Aztec and Mayan sites comprise one of the country's strongest attractions to visitors. And even those who choose a strictly beach vacation on the Caribbean coast have plenty of chances to take a look at Mexico's heroic past.

From as early as 1500 BC, the region witnessed a succession of city-states of extraordinary wealth and achievements. The first was the Olmec civilization, centered at the place now known as San Lorenzo (east of the present Mexico City). By 800 BC, the Olmecs' focus had moved southeast along the Gulf Coast to the island site now known as La Venta. Over the next four hundred years, the Olmecs became the most sophisticated society in the Americas.

Traces of Olmec traditions can be found in the next two great civilizations, Teotihuacán and the Maya. Teotihuacán became

established around the first century AD, about 30 miles from the present heart of Mexico City. The magnificent relics of the biggest pre-Hispanic city still stand.

In parallel, the Maya created the most articulate civilization further east. Their influence spread across the Yucatán into present-day Belize, Guatemala and Honduras, and for seven centuries they were one of the world's most advanced peoples.

Descendants of the Maya constitute one of the main groups of the indigenous peoples living in Mexico today.

Both the Maya and Teotihuacán declined as the first millennium AD ended. The next significant society was Aztec, who moved from the northwest into central Mexico around 1300. Within a century, much of present-day Mexico was controlled by an empire whose heart was located at the center of the current capital. This was the power base captured by Hernán Cortés and his Conquistadores in 1521, after some bloody conflict.

The invaders plundered the great civilization and enslaved its

people. For the next three centuries, Mexico was a heavily exploited colony of Spain. Inspired by the revolutionary spirit sweeping Latin America, and helped by Napoleon Bonaparte's occupation of Spain, rebels began the campaign for independence. This was achieved in 1821, whereupon a series of leaders whose chief characteristic was instability (both mental and political) took charge. A series of military setbacks saw much Mexican territory – notably Texas – ceded to the United States. Apart from a period of French occupation from 1864 to 1867, power fell into the hands of a succession of autocrats of varying degrees of benevolence. Some would say that this pattern persists today. After a decade-long civil war that ended in 1920, the political force that was to dominate for the rest of the century took shape. The Partido Revolucionario Institucional has presided over dramatic changes and a surge in population, though the elections in 1997 showed signs of its power base beginning to crumble.

Get Around

in Mexico
and Central America

The all-in-one travel and language guide

Marisol de Lafuente and Simon Calder

Library of Congress Cataloging-in-Publication Data
is available from the United States Library of Congress

Photographs
All photographs by Chris Caldicott, except the following:

Sylvia Cordaiy: p12, 13
Luke Finn: spine
Getty Images: p10(b), 17(b), 26, 28, 29(t)
Robert Harding Picture Library: p20, 21
The Image Bank: p10(t), 11, 14, 16, 25(t)
Life File: p15, 29(b)
Pictor International – London: back (br), p17(t), 24, 25(b)
Rex Interstock: p27
Zefa Pictures: cover, p3(b)
Cover design by Carroll Associates
Map: Malcolm Porter

This edition published by Passport Books
An imprint of NTC/Contemporary Publishing Company
4255 West Touhy Avenue
Lincolnwood (Chicago), Illinois 60646-1975 U.S.A.

Published in cooperation with BBC Enterprises Ltd. "BBC" and the
BBC logotype are trademarks of the British Broadcasting Corporation
and are used under license.
© BBC Worldwide Ltd 1998.
All rights reserved. No part of this book may be reproduced,
stored in a retrieval system, or transmitted in any form
or by any means, electronic, mechanical, photocopying,
recording, or otherwise, without the prior permission of
NTC/Contemporary Publishing Company.

Printed in the United Kingdom

International Standard Book Number: 0-8442-0150-2 book
International Standard Book Number: 0-8442-0161-8 package
1 3 5 7 9 11 12 10 8 6 4 2

INSIDER'S GUIDE

The Mexican people

Any attempt briefly to characterize a nation of almost 100 million people is doomed to be simplistic, but as far as the visitor is concerned, the principal feature of most Mexicans is their innate friendliness and genuine hospitality. This is as true of the rapidly expanding middle class in the capital as it is of the less fortunate in a relatively poor province such as Oaxaca or Chiapas.

Within the soul of the typical *mestizo* (mixed-blood) Mexican resides Hispanic passion and Indian stoicism, with a dash of Caribbean spice and a flash of *Norteamericano* (North American) style. While the *mañana* reputation for a certain cheerful tardiness is not entirely justified, in less developed parts of Mexico you can expect a relaxed attitude towards time-keeping. Many Mexicans also take a relaxed view of the dominant religion, Catholicism. The influence of the Church has declined significantly in recent years, as it has elsewhere in the Spanish-speaking world.

Mass tourism has inevitably distorted the relationship between host and guest in the most heavily visited parts of Mexico, but by stepping off the tourist trail, however briefly, you can be sure of meeting friendly people.

Mexico's geography and climate

The first thing the visitor should appreciate is the sheer size of the country. From Tijuana in the extreme northwest to Cancún at the tip of the Yucatán Peninsula is an east–west distance of nearly 2,000 miles, straddling three time zones.

Within this vast area, there is a huge range of terrain. The main feature, however, is the amount of high ground. A good proportion of the country is above a mile high, and much of this is mountainous.

The main spine, the Sierra Madre Occidental, is a continuation of the US and Canadian Rocky Mountains. It reaches its highest point, Popocatépetl, close to Mexico City. This area marks the convergence with the Sierra Madre Oriental that stretches down the eastern part of the country. A third significant range, the Sierra Madre del Sur, separates the south coast from the interior.

Besides these imposing ranges, there is a wide range of more gentle topography. The Yucatán Peninsula is a mostly flat area that protrudes deep into the Caribbean. At the western extreme, Baja California is a rocky finger stretching for 750 miles into the Pacific. The coastal areas of the central trunk of the country are mostly low lying, with some spectacularly good beaches.

Given the size of Mexico, it is reckless to generalize about climate. In most parts of the country, though, there are broadly two seasons. From May to October, it is hot and wet, especially on the eastern coast. This Caribbean side of the country – and particularly the Yucatán Peninsula, where many popular resorts are located – is prone to storms bordering on hurricanes from July to September. From November to April, temperatures and rainfall both ease.

Many inland areas, from Oaxaca in the south to Juárez in the north, and including the Distrito Federal where Mexico City is located, are relatively cool and dry throughout the year. Baja California, too, receives much less rain than you might expect from its position protruding into the Pacific.

At the Caribbean and Pacific resorts, warm clothing is likely to remain unpacked for your stay; humidity tends to be the main problem. But if you are visiting high-altitude areas such as Mexico City, be prepared for chilly mornings and evenings. Bus travelers should also bundle up, because of the powerful air-conditioning systems beloved of Mexican bus drivers.

Currency/changing money

Visitors from the United States, Canada, and Western Europe generally find prices in Mexico to be very favorable. The local currency, the peso, has taken something of a beating in the 1990s and is relatively weak against the US dollar, which is the dominant foreign currency in Mexico.

Confusingly, the symbol used for the peso is $ – almost exactly the same as for the US dollar. In border areas, where many prices are shown in American currency for the benefit of day-trippers, it will not always be clear which is intended. If you are not sure, ask *¿Moneda nacional?* – literally "National money?," ie Mexican currency.

Changing money at banks, bureaux de change (marked *Casa de Cambio* or simply *Cambio*, meaning "change") and hotel desks is easy as long as you have US dollars (cash or traveler's checks). You may find it difficult to change other currencies away from the big cities and resort areas – Canadian dollars are the most widely recognized.

Every Mexican knows the peso–dollar rate, and some street dealers will offer "special deals." One of the many dangers of such transactions is that you may receive obsolete currency; the peso has gone through high inflation and revaluation in the past decade, and some villains pass off old notes and coins to unsuspecting tourists.

Credit cards are now ubiquitous and are accepted in a wide range of hotels, restaurants and stores. Some enterprises deal in US dollars for the purposes of credit-card transactions; be sure that the currency details correspond with

INSIDER'S GUIDE

what you are expecting.

Every sizeable town has a range of automatic teller machines (ATMs), and if you need quick cash it is well worth trying your credit or bank card on one of these – called a *caja permanente* or a *cajero automático*. Given the glitches that continue to afflict international payment systems, being able to get money from "hole-in-the-wall" machines should not be relied upon.

Visas and entry requirements

Rules for foreigners vary, depending on nationality and the extent of the trip – a quick hop across the border from the United States, or a longer expedition. Problems frequently arise in US border areas, when it is assumed that everyone arriving is only a day-tripper.

American and Canadian citizens do not require passports to visit Mexico, though one is advisable for anyone planning extended travel; in out-of-the-way places, a driver's license or birth certificate may not be regarded as a sufficiently good assurance of identity. Furthermore, problems may arise when re-entering the US or Canada.

Other nationalities require a passport but not a visa. Every traveler who is staying for more than 72 hours, and/or traveling beyond the US-Mexico border zone, must have a tourist card. Officially, this is called a *Forma Migratoria de Turista*, but everyone refers to it as a *tarjeta de turista*.

If you are flying directly into Mexico, then the airline will probably supply one of these. You fill it in, and the immigration official at the airport of arrival will assign a length of stay (up to 180 days) and stamp the form.

If you are traveling by land, then you should obtain the card from the immigration office immediately upon arrival. As mentioned above, travelers arriving from across the land border with the United States are presumed to be day-trippers. Unless you seek out the right office before traveling deeper into Mexico, you could land in trouble when you try to leave.

Mexico City

A high-altitude city of 20 million people drenched in a fearful smog might not seem to command a place at the top of a wish-list of possible destinations – or indeed anywhere. Yet Mexico City turns out to possess a calm and civilized soul, which rewards those with the modicum of determination required to seek it out. Imagine a slightly bedraggled version of Paris, and you are nearly there. Handsome, low-rise apartment buildings mingle with glamorous flourishes by 19th-century architects and the odd eruption of modern Mexico brashness. You will often see Mexico City referred to as "DF." This stands for Distrito Federal, *a "capital territory" akin to the District of Columbia in the US.*

Don't miss

The Zócalo, the magnificent plaza that has been the heart of the capital – and the country – since Aztec times. A gigantic Mexican flag flies over the vast main square, where life is always intense. On the north and east faces are two of Mexico City's greatest sights, with several others in the immediate vicinity.

The Cathedral Mexico City's Catedral Metropolitana is as breathtaking in its diversity as it is in its scale, occupying the entire northern side of the Zócalo. It was begun half a century after the Conquest and finished 240 years later, during which a rich confusion of styles was employed. Since then, huge cracks in the façade testify to the geological instability of Mexico City. A repair effort called the *Corrección Geométrica* is underway.

The Palacio Nacional Another monumental edifice, taking up the eastern face of the Zócalo. New

MEXICO CITY

arrivals can brush up on Mexican history with Diego Rivera's dramatic mural on the development of the nation.
A walk around the ruins of the Templo Mayor Mexico City's origins

A drink on the 43rd floor of the Torre Latinoamericana, Mexico's tallest building – preferably at sunset when the whole sprawling mass of Mexico City takes on a strange orange hue.

Rivera's Sueño de Tarde Dominical en la Alameda

are still being excavated from five centuries of dereliction at the hands of the Spanish. The Templo Mayor was the center of the Aztec world and, together with its excellent museum, you get a strong sense of pre-Colombian life.
A wander through the atrium of the Gran Hotel de la Ciudad de México, a century-old palace of Art Nouveau that will make you gasp at its scale and style.
The Museo Nacional de Antropología, the most impressive museum in all of Latin America. Everything that could be salvaged from the Conquest has been assembled here, from the tablets used to calculate the Aztec calendar to the dazzling images of the Mayans.
Wall paintings at the Museo Mural Diego Rivera, notably the heroic *Sueño de Tarde Dominical en la Alameda* (Dream of Sunday afternoon in the Alameda) depicting important figures from Cortés to Rivera himself.

Clubs and bars

Casa Rasta (Calle Florencia 44), a reggae bar which, around midnight, becomes the rowdiest place in the Zona Rosa.
El Chato (Calle Londres 117), in contrast, is a relaxed piano bar.
El Taller (Calle Florencia 37), mainly for gay men.
Restaurante-Bar León (through the arcade at Avenida República de Brasil 5) is much more of a disco than a restaurant or bar, and is possibly the best salsa venue in the city.

Have coffee or a snack in

Café de Tacuba (Calle Tacuba 28), a turn-of-the-century metropolitan palace.
Café La Blanca (across the road at Calle 5 de Mayo 40), where tourists mingle with office workers over coffee, cakes and cerveza.

INSIDER'S GUIDE

Euseba (in the Zona Rosa at Calle Hamburgo 159b), where Mexico City's polite society meets for tea and gossip.
La Dulcería de Celaya (Calle 5 de Mayo 39), the grandest candy store you will ever experience.
Pastelería Ideal (Avenida 16 de Septiembre and Calle de Gante), a palace of patisserie where the cakes and pastries will defeat anyone's diet.

Have a meal in

Bolívar 12 (its name is its address), a cheerfully theatrical restaurant which boasts 130 varieties of Tequila.
Cicero's (Calle Londres 195), one of the world's most stylish oyster bars, with prices to match.
La Opera (Calle 5 de Mayo 10), a crowded Baroque barn of a place where there are plenty of posers.
Sanborn's (Avenida Madero 4) – part of a quasi-American chain, but this branch, swathed in tiles, has the most delightful courtyard setting in the Casa de los Azulejos, an 18th-century mansion covered in tiles.

Children's Mexico City

The Mexican capital is home to around eight million children, but that does not mean it is an ideal place for young foreign visitors. Children are more likely to be affected by the city's appalling pollution, and may find the intensity of street life distressing. Having said that, Mexicans tend to be thoroughly indulgent towards foreign children – blond and blue-eyed or red-haired children in particular.

The Bosque de Chapultepec is an ideal park for children, especially the Parque Zoológico – one of the more humane and well-organized of Latin America's zoos. *The News* includes a "For Children" section in its events listings.

Transportation

Taxis
The standard Mexico City taxi is a worn-out Volkswagen Beetle, with its front passenger seat removed to facilitate entry for passengers and their luggage, or a (slightly) more modern Nissan. It is painted either yellow or green, the latter signifying that it runs on unleaded gas.

Until you become familiar with the pace of life in the capital, there is a lot to be said for sticking to taxis. Noisy and cramped though they might be, they are extremely easy to find and pretty cheap. Insist that the driver charges according to the meter (*taxímetro*). There is no need to tip, though some drivers have come

MEXICO CITY

to expect foreign visitors at least to round up the fare to the nearest peso.

Subway
Stations are indicated by the symbol of a curiously stylised "m." Buy a ticket (*boleto*) from the booth and feed it into the slot on the turnstile; there is a flat fare to any station on the nine lines. The direction of the trains is shown by *Dirección* plus the name of the last station on the line.

Useful Subway stations
Terminal Aérea (line 5): for the airport. Note that Boulevard Puerto Aéreo, on line 1, is nowhere near the passenger terminals.
Zócalo (line 2): for the center of the city, including the Palacio Nacional and the Cathedral.
Insurgentes (line 1): for the Zona Rosa, the upscale shopping and entertainment area.
Auditorio (line 7): for the Bosque de Chapultepec.

City buses and *peseros*
The short-term visitor to Mexico City will find the bus system confusing. There are full-size buses (run by the local authority, with the same flat fare as the subway) and smaller minibuses known as *peseros* (privately run and slightly more expensive). Even if you know the route number that you want, a frequent problem is that buses stop short of the usual terminus, or depart from the normal route. In addition, they can be extremely crowded at rush hours.

Under your own steam
Pedestrians need to take extreme care negotiating the traffic in Mexico City, and beware of uneven pavements (sidewalks), open manholes, etc. Only an unnecessarily reckless person would ever consider bicycling in Mexico City, though some cycle rickshaws (*Bici-Taxi*) now circulate, allowing you to be pedaled around at bus-exhaust level.

A day trip from Mexico City

Teotihuacán
"The place where men become gods" is how the name translates. Mesoamerican civilization planned that this transition should take place in suitably heavenly surroundings. So 21 centuries ago, the Avenue of the Dead was laid out. The miraculous Pyramid of the Sun and its smaller, younger sibling, the Pyramid of the Moon are the most powerful sights.

Teotihuacán

Tijuana and Baja California

*F*or many visitors, the sprawling city of Tijuana is the first taste of Mexico. Tijuana is no more representative of Mexico than New York City typifies the US, but – as millions of day-trippers discover each year – it has a cheap and cheerful charm. Stretching like a slender finger south into the Pacific Ocean, Baja California is a region of rugged beauty. Its 800-mile extent contains historic Jesuit missions and isolated fishing communities dotted around a spine of arid mountains.

Don't miss

Tijuana, the fastest-growing city in Mexico

- Avenida Revolución, the manic main street that caters to US visitors 24 hours a day. Locals and day-trippers call it "La Revo."
- Frontón Palacio Jai Alai, the biggest landmark on La Revo. The gaudy exterior conceals a serious sports arena, where the Mexican embellishment of the ancient Basque game of pelota is played daily.
- Vinícola L A Cetto, the most accessible winery in Baja. The peninsula produces some of Mexico's best wines, and visitors pay a nominal sum to sample a good range.
- Mercado Hidalgo, a strictly Mexican contrast to the kitsch retailing along La Revo.

Cabo San Lucas

TIJUANA AND BAJA CALIFORNIA

Rosarito Until the 1848 Treaty of Guadalupe Hidalgo that ended the Mexican–American War, Rosarito marked the frontier between Baja and Alta California. Nowadays, it is an unashamed beach resort.

Ensenada If you thought Tijuana acted as the safety valve for the excesses of young Californians, think again. The port city of Ensenada attracts huge partying crowds from north of the border. But some attractive nearby scenery, and the prospect of whale-watching trips, makes it a worthwhile stop.

of the "real" Baja, unsullied by mass tourism.
■ Guerrero Negro: an old whaling port, where the main industry is now watching, rather than catching, the mammals.
■ Santa Rosalía: located where the Transpeninsular Highway strikes the eastern shore of Baja, Santa Rosalía is actually a copper-mining town established by the French.

Cabo San Lucas

Tour of the main sights of Baja California
■ Highway 1 begins at the US border and winds its way south through many of Baja's places of interest. Driving conditions are good, and the route is also plied by plenty of buses.
■ San Quintín: a concentration of bays and beaches punctured by volcanoes, with traces of a 19th-century British attempt at commercial settlement.
■ El Rosario: as you head south, this sleepy market town is the first taste

Though the ore is now exhausted, the settlement retains plenty of Gallic influence. Ferries sail from here across the Sea of Cortés to Guaymas on the "mainland."
■ La Paz: another crossing point, La Paz contrives to be the biggest city in southern Baja while retaining a serene sense of antiquity. It lies on an attractive bay, across which you see fine sunsets – quite an achievement for an east-coast town.
■ Cabo San Lucas: regarded by many Alta Californians (residents of the US state of California) as a good approximation to paradise, the resort at the southernmost tip of Baja offers fine beaches and strange rock formations.

Puerto Vallarta

*S*outh and west of the country's mountainous spine, Pacific Mexico comprises a collection of historic cities and attractive resorts, interleaved by spectacular scenery. Thousands of visitors choose Puerto Vallarta as the optimum resort, offering as it does attractive beaches centred on an old colonial core, with lovely coves further afield.

Don't miss

The beaches, which form an alluring arc of ten miles around the bay, interrupted by the Río Cuale that divides Puerto Vallarta.
Isla Cuale, the long, thin island in the middle of the river, with a

modest museum at the western end.
Plaza Principal, the main square at the heart of the old town, on the north side of the river.
A stroll along Calle Morelos and back down Calle Juárez, lined with sophisticated shops, art galleries – and timeshare solicitors.
The Mercado Municipal, four blocks inland and just north of the island, which will help you remember you are still in Mexico.

Have a drink, snack or meal in

Any of the cafés and bars that line the Malecón, the promenade north of the Río Cuale. A cocktail while the sun goes down is particularly popular.
Pie in the Sky (Calle Basilio Badillo 278), a bakery where the main ingredient is indulgence.
Planet Hollywood (north of the river at Avenida Ordaz 652), which has replaced the Hard Rock Café as the most sought-after place in town.
Puerto Nuevo (Calle Basilio Badillo 284), almost next door, where good, healthy seafood is the order of the day.
Restaurant Nanahuatzin (south of the river at Olas Altas 336), a chic place specializing in a mix of dishes

based on ancient and modern recipes.

Children's Puerto Vallarta

The resort was designed to be child friendly. Many of the visitors to Puerto Vallarta are on "all-inclusive" deals, with plenty of activities included in the price of the package. For variation, there are plenty of beaches to choose from and a good range of attendant attractions.

Puerto Vallarta's transportation

Buses are cheap and frequent. Taxis operate according to a complicated system of zones, and some visitors complain that this results in higher fares than elsewhere in Mexico. The ideal way to travel around, though, is on the network of water taxis that operates from Los Muertos pier south of the Río Cuales. These serve various points around the Bahía de Banderas.

Day trips from Puerto Vallarta

Mismaloya If you have seen John Huston's film *The Night of the Iguana*, you may be surprised to learn that it was filmed only seven miles southwest of the center of Puerto Vallarta. Although Mismaloya is now far from idyllic, the movie connection makes it a good day out.
Boca de Tomatlán, further around the broad crescent of the bay, is much more unspoiled.
Yelapa, still further west, is where many of the cruises from Puerto Vallarta end up, and is correspondingly commercialized. To escape the crowds, head inland to the hills.

Las Animas beach

Guadalajara

*U*nlike Mexico City, Guadalajara was founded by the Spanish on an entirely new site rather than at an existing settlement. Visitors to Guadalajara who have also been to Spain often comment that the capital of Jalisco State is really a Mexicanized Spanish city. Anyone arriving from Mexico City is likely to regard Guadalajara as a more civilized and genteel place than the national capital. And as Mexico's second-largest city, Guadalajara has a wide range of attractions for travelers.

Don't miss

The Cathedral, whose two tall towers mark the center of the city. Outside, it is a real mix of architecture; the interior is heavy with columns and gilt.

Dawn at Mercado Libertad, watching Mexico's liveliest market blearily come to life.

A morning at the Tequila Sauza distillery in the western outskirts, which offers free tours (in English) washed down by free samples.

An afternoon at the Parque del Mirador, a viewpoint overlooking the vast canyon known as the Barranca de Oblatos – not quite as impressive as the Copper Canyon, but much easier to reach.

An evening at the Plaza de los Mariachis, a permanent venue for some of Mexico's best troubadours.

The Palacio de Gobierno, whose walls bear murals by José Clemente Orozco that have resonances of the work of Diego Rivera.

Paying your respects to the Doce Hombres Ilustres, statues of twelve illustrious Guadalajaran citizens standing guard over a Rotunda just north of the cathedral.

Checking out the people checking in at the Hotel de Mendoza (just north of Plaza Hidalgo), a converted convent that is now Guadalajara's most characteristic accommodation.

Strolling in the Parque Agua Azul – don't expect too much blue water, but this broad park is a welcome oasis from the city streets.

The Instituto Cultural Cabañas, a former orphanage whose neo-classical columns conceal a maze of courtyards – 23 in all.

The Templo de San Francisco, a spacious yet intricate church that is almost as old as the city.

Have a drink, snack or meal in

Café Madrid (Avenida Juárez 264), a Mexican version of an American diner. Moderate prices.

Villa Madrid (Calle López Cotilla 223) – no relation to the above, but a cheap, cheerful vegetarian restaurant.

Café Quetzal (Avenida Unión 236) levies a cover charge, but that is to pay for the live music every night. Drinks are expensive, but you are not hassled to down them rapidly.

Hotel Francés (behind the Palacio de Gobierno, Calle Maestranza 35) The piano bar in the lobby is a cool, pleasant and central place to meet.
Restaurant la Feria (Avenida Corona 291), excellent location (on the east side of the Templo); short menu, good value.

Children's Guadalajara

Young visitors are very well provided for. The Museo Infantil, on the east side of the Parque Agua Azul, is a thoughtful, hands-on collection, though its short opening hours (Monday to Friday, mornings only) can be frustrating. The Zoo, to the north of the city, is large and attractive. Close by is the Selva Mágica, a modest amusement park, and the Planetarium – where under-twelves are admitted free.

Transportation

The public transportation system seems more orderly than in Mexico City, with a good network of buses, a small but efficient subway and taxis that do not get too snarled up in traffic.

City buses
Pay the driver when you board. The usual city buses are amplified on main routes by some combi minibuses.

Useful bus routes
Number 60: linking the city center with the railway station and the old bus station.
Number 275: (and 275a): city center to the new bus station, a half-hour haul south-east.

Subway
A simple cross of two lines, running north–south and east–west. Stations are marked with a large T. Tokens for the flat fare are sold at station booths.

Taxis
Drivers in Guadalajara do not always use meters, instead relying on a system of zones. Establish the price before you get in.

Day trips from Guadalajara

Tonalá Just beyond the eastern suburbs, the first "proper" town you reach is a craft center, which also has an interesting ceramics museum.
Tequila The home of Mexico's national drink is 31 miles west of Guadalajara, and if the wind is in the right direction then you can smell it well before you arrive. The two main brands are José Cuervo and Tequila Sauza, both of which offer free tours of their distilleries.
Lago de Chapala Mexico's largest lake stretches for 50 miles to the south and east of Guadalajara. The main town, Chapala, is packed with day-trippers at weekends; during the rest of the week, there is a large population of anglophone expatriates, following in the footsteps of D. H. Lawrence who lived and wrote here for a while. Traveling further around the shore allows you to leave the crowds behind.

Acapulco

*F**ew modern visitors to Acapulco are aware of the deep historical significance of this magnificent Pacific bay. Until Mexico achieved independence, Acapulco was New Spain's link with its Asian colony of the Philippines. Goods were shipped from Manila to the port of Acapulco, then taken on a long overland route via Mexico City to Veracruz for onward shipment to Europe.*

When Mexico became independent, the importance and wealth of Acapulco went into sharp decline, reviving in the 20th century when it was at the forefront of the development of Mexican beach tourism. Since the Cuban Revolution in 1959 diverted US tourists from Cuba to other destinations, the resort has been immensely popular.

Don't miss

The fearless divers of La Quebrada, one of the most awesome spectacles in Mexico. What began as a demonstration of machismo has become a tourist attraction: each day, a group of high-divers plunge from rocks just west of the old town into a narrow crevice.

The beaches protected within the Bahía de Acapulco, which – heading west from the old town – are named Hornos, Hornitos, Condesa and Icacos. Watch out, however, for the rather treacherous waters off Condesa.

The bays of Caletilla and Caleta Gentler waters and prettier surroundings than those within Acapulco Bay.

The Fuerte de San Diego, the huge 17th-century fortress standing guard over the port where galleons once arrived from Asia. It now houses Acapulco's historical museum.

ACAPULCO

A sunset cruise in, out and around the bay. Intense competition keeps prices reasonable, though after a few days you may tire of solicitors trying to entice you onboard.

Have a drink, snack or meal in

El Galeón, a block west of the Zócalo, an endearing mock-colonial mansion offering good food at reasonable prices.
Super Soya on Jesús Carranza, close to the Zócalo; good vegetarian snacks and juices, plus granola and ginseng.
El Taco Rico (Benito Juárez), the best of the cheap and cheerful cafés on the fringes of the Zócalo.
Woolworth's, the cafeteria of choice for many locals; good fixed-rate meals all day.

Children's Acapulco

Apart from the beach, most visiting children seem content to make the most of the Parque Papagayo amusement area, stretching back from the shore east of the old town. Transportation within the park is provided by a miniature railway and chair lifts, while activities range from boating to rollerblading. Further around the bay, Cici is a

La Quebrada

combination water sports/marine life park.

Transportion

The airport is a long way east of the resort, but an efficient system of collective taxis will get you to your hotel quickly and economically. Buses race (usually literally) up and down La Costera, the main strip, every few minutes. Fares for taxis should always be negotiated in advance.

Day trips from Acapulco

Pie de la Cuesta The main reason for visitors to leave the confines of Acapulco itself is to seek out yet more beaches, and this ribbon of sand, six miles northwest, is the best of the bunch. Always observe the warning flags; the currents are often dangerous.
Puerto Marqués In the opposite direction, this quiet cove about twelve miles southeast is a good antidote to the beach life of the Bahía.
Revolcadero If you fly direct to Acapulco, this could be your first sight of a beach – it is close to the airport. A long, flat stretch of sand is fully exposed to the might of the Pacific, making for good surfing and challenging swimming.

Oaxaca

Many travelers nominate Oaxaca as their favorite Mexican city. Atmospheric Spanish colonial architecture, vestiges of pre-Columbian life and a quarter of a million residents are compressed into a compact, lively mountain city. Most visitors seem to leave with a tangible reminder of their stay – Oaxaca produces the best handicrafts in Mexico.

Don't miss

The Zócalo, a fine main square fringed by cafés and steeped in history. The two dominant buildings, the Palacio de Gobierno and Cathedral, are worth investigating, but most people simply relax and take in the street life.
Iglesia de Santo Domingo, whose heavy stone walls have withstood two massive earthquakes to preserve the most impressive colonial church in the city. Behind it, you find quiet gardens and a lively cultural center.
Learning about the Mixtecs and Zapotecs at the Museo Regional de Oaxaca, adjacent to Santo Domingo.
Climbing the stairs along Calle Mier y Terán, adjacent to the Basilica de La Soledad, to reveal excellent views of the city.
A more ambitious ascent of the Escalera del Fortín (from Calle Crespo in the northwest of the city) to Cerro del Fortín, a hill topped by a giant cross.
Strolling along Calle Alcalá, mercifully free of traffic and full of shoppers and promenaders.
A performance in the Teatro Macedonio Alcalá, a startling confection of a theater on Calle Independencia.
Visiting the home of Benito Juárez, now the Museo Casa de Juárez. Four times President of Mexico, Juárez steered the country through

Monte Albán

OAXACA

the turmoil of the mid-19th century.
Shopping in the twin markets of Juárez and 20 de Noviembre.
A festival, of which Oaxaca is endowed with more than its fair share. July and December are the best months.

Have a drink, snack or meal in

The Zócalo, where a dozen cafés and restaurants compete and mariachi musicians ask for tips.
Café Candela (Calle Allende 211), for drinks, food or music in any combination, in a colonial setting.

August 31, when household pets are dressed up and taken to the church of La Merced to be blessed. For the rest of the year, events and activities for children are hard to find.

Transportation

The city has the usual array of raucous old buses and battered "combi" minibuses, but Oaxaca is so compact one could walk everywhere – even, unusually, to the bus stations.

Day trips from Oaxaca

Mitla

Restaurant del Vitral (Calle Guerrero 201), for a range of local dishes – including insects – served in sumptuous surroundings. Expensive but worthwhile.
Restaurant Flor de Loto del Sureste (Calle Portfiro Díaz 217), a reliable vegetarian place with reasonable prices.

Children's Oaxaca

Because Oaxaca is a relatively small city, it is not as well equipped with diversions for children as other places. Young visitors will adore the Blessing of Animals festival each

Monte Albán Zapotec culture is less celebrated than Mayan and Aztec civilizations, but this site – a short way west of Oaxaca – reveals an extraordinarily sophisticated pre-Colombian city, at its most powerful around 500AD.
Teotitlán del Valle If you have not spent all your spare cash in Oaxaca, then the dramatic textiles that are woven in this pretty village 20 miles east of the city should part you from the remainder.
Mitla The faces in the streets of the present town are mostly Zapotec, descendants of those who built the city around a millennium ago.

19

Veracruz

*T*his city of (at least) half a million people has long been Mexico's lifeline to the rest of the world. It was here that Hernán Cortés first landed to begin the Conquest in 1519, and for more than two centuries Veracruz held a monopoly on trade with Spain – a privilege that earned the city repeated attacks from privateers. Today, it is a cheerfully animated place and though there is plenty to keep visitors occupied, it is not yet an especially popular destination for foreign tourists.

Don't miss

The fort of San Juan de Ulúa, guarding the port. The *castillo* dangles from a causeway to the north of the city, giving an excellent overview for new arrivals to the port. Within the fort there is a fascinating warren of passageways, tunnels and dungeons.
The Plaza de Armas (also called the *zócalo*), the big main square in the middle of the city – at its energetic best each evening.
Ambling along the Malecón, the waterside boulevard.
Seeing the location purporting to be the birthplace of the Mexican Constitution, the lighthouse (*faro*) named for General Venustiano Carranza, one of the authors.
Riding up to La Prueba, a factory where you see the leaf-to-lips lifecycle of the cigar.
Climbing aboard the *Santa María* – not the actual ship that carried Columbus from Spain on his historic first voyage, but a replica constructed with the help of the original plans.

Pico de Orizaba

Shopping at the Plaza de las Artesanías, for a better class of crafts than you find in many places.

Have a drink, snack or meal in

One of the stands upstairs at the fish market (on Calle Landero y Cos between Serdán and Arista), filled with dozens of vendors selling ultra-fresh seafood at low prices.
La Parroquia (Avenida Independencia 105), an institution; get a friendly local to explain the *café con leche* ritual. Moderate prices. A second version, **La Parroquia II**, is opposite the harbor.
Café El Profeta (corner of Calles Juárez and Madero), for tasty vegetarian food at reasonable prices.
Panificadora París (corner of Avenida 5 de Mayo and Calle Mario Molina), serving the most tempting pastries in the East.

Children's Veracruz

There is only one destination in town: the magnificent aquarium on the shore east of the city center. Sharks and turtles are the main attractions in the tanks, while children are encouraged to touch everything from coral to conch shells.

Day trips from Veracruz

Playa Mocambo With the beach some way out of town (five miles south), this is best regarded as a day-trip. Fine sand and safe water await those who catch one of the frequent buses along the highway.
Boca del Río A short way south of Mocambo, where the banks of the river in question are lined with seafood restaurants.
Isla de Sacrificios, reached by boat from the harbor. Human sacrifices no longer take place, and instead it is a good venue for some gentle hiking or serious diving.

Chichén Itzá

The Yucatán

If any region can be considered "Mexico in microcosm," then it would have to be the Yucatán Peninsula: ancient civilizations of amazing complexity, vestiges of the Spanish colonialism that supplanted Mayan society, and some of the best beaches on the Caribbean.

Don't miss

Mérida, perhaps the most perfectly preserved colonial city in Mexico.
■ The Plaza Mayor, as stimulating as it is symmetrical.
■ The Palacio de Gobierno, containing some especially powerful murals.
■ The lobby of the Gran Hotel, which could have come straight from a film set.

Mérida

■ Trying a Panama hat on for size at Sombrerería "el Becaleño" (Calle 65 number 483).
■ Splashing out on dinner at the Restaurant El Tucho (Calle 60 number 482).

The Ruta Maya The "Maya Road" is not a single highway as such, but a figure-of-eight route around the most significant historic sites of the Mayan people. The top half circumscribes the Yucatán Peninsula, passing through Mérida and Cancún. The bottom half of the eight circles around the Mexican state of Chiapas then into Guatemala, brushes against Honduras, then continues through Guatemala and Belize to the Mexican city of Chetumal, where it joins the top half of the route.

The most striking Mayan structures are the pyramids, which tower above the low-lying surroundings. These differ substantially from those in Egypt: they are more steeply raked, and are of much more simple construction (dressed stone over a core of rubble), topped by a temple.

Chichén Itzá, Mexico's most complete and compelling Mayan site. The main Pyramid of Kukulcán towers above the surrounding countryside, giving spectacular views of the ancient city. You can wander around ball courts that predate tennis by a millennium, study the gruesome Temple of Skulls and wonder at the skills of those who built such a place.

Uxmal Although this site, south of Mérida, does not have the scale of Chichén Itzá, neither is it a Mayan theme park on the circuit of Cancún tourists. Compressed into a few acres you find a towering pyramid whose ascent is scarier than traveling on any Mexican road, a pre-Catholic convent and an archaic civic center.

Tulum The spectacular location of this site, on the cliff tops overlooking the Caribbean, compensates for a less impressive collection of ruins than Uxmal or Chichén Itzá.

Cancún The stories about Mexico's favorite resort are legion. Some say that it was designed by computer to maximize the revenue from sun-seeking foreigners. Others say the place is a misrepresentation of the real Mexico, or that the large number of all-inclusive resorts are tarnishing relations with the residents. While there is a grain of truth in each of these, most visitors

Cancún

find the place tremendous fun.

There is something for everyone, from slices of ancient Mayan civilizations in the Archaeological Museum and even the grounds of the Sheraton to karaoke bars and endless pizza joints. To stay in touch with the real Mexico, you need only wander into the town center and immerse yourself in the market.

Day trips from Cancún

Isla Mujeres The style of life on this long, slim, vacation island is much more relaxed than in Cancún, and it is an ideal alternative to its intense commercialism. Boats leave regularly to the island, whose western beaches are excellent. The town, is well worth exploring too.

Playa del Carmen The beaches are good at this mainland resort, which is less developed than Cancún.

Cancún beach

Central America and the Caribbean

Travelers who have enjoyed the people, culture and landscapes of Mexico can quickly become addicted to Latin American life. South of the Mexican border, the six much smaller Spanish-speaking countries of Central America lack the relative wealth and infrastructure of Mexico, but provide many new dimensions for the visitor. Traces of Mayan culture can be found along the Ruta Maya in the east of Guatemala and into Honduras, while the Pacific side boasts many fine beaches as well as some spectacular volcanoes. This section focuses on the two most popular Central American nations, Guatemala and Costa Rica, plus the largest island in the Caribbean – Cuba.

Lake Atitlán

Guatemala

On a journey south from Mexico into the rest of Spanish-speaking America, the first nation you encounter is strikingly attractive in terms of both scenery and culture. Guatemala is the size of the state of Louisiana and is shaped like a piece from a jigsaw puzzle, wedged awkwardly between Mexico, Belize and Honduras. It is the only Central American country where indigenous Mayan Indian people are in the majority; Mayan traditions are most vividly conveyed in their bright, hand-woven textiles. Three decades of bloody civil war ended in 1996, opening up territory previously off-limits to visitors.

Don't miss

Guatemala City, the modern capital. Even though this earthquake-bruised city of 1.6 million people initially appears devoid of saving graces, persevere. Guatemala City is a good starting place for further travels. In Museo Popol Vuh it has an excellent archaeological museum, and the remains of what was once a vast Mayan city, Kaminaljuyú, are on the fringe of the modern capital.
Antigua Guatemala, the old Spanish capital. This was the first place in the Americas to be laid out on a grid pattern, setting the style for cities everywhere from New York to Santiago de Chile. Abandoned as center of government in the 17th century as too earthquake-prone, Antigua has retained its (literally) crumbling colonial integrity, and happily accommodates the large numbers of people learning Spanish as a foreign language in the city.
Lake Atitlán, a mile high and the closest approximation to Shangri-La in the Americas. The view from the main lakeside town of Panajachel is of a graceful pair of volcanoes, Atitlán and Tolimán, mirrored in the calm, cold, shimmering water. An hour's boat ride across the lake takes you to the tranquil village of Santiago Atitlán, which comes to colorful life in the vibrant market.
Tikal, arguably the most complete and impressive Mayan city of all, rescued only within the last 150 years from the thick tropical jungle of the Petén – the region that protrudes into Mexico. Only a fraction of the estimated 3,000 buildings have been uncovered, but they include the breathtaking Plaza Mayor, dominated by the pyramid known as the Jaguar Temple.
Flores, close to Tikal, a colonial gem of a town impeccably located on an island in Lake Petén Itzá. Few places in the Americas are so serene.

Costa Rica

In contrast to its immediate neighbors, Costa Rica has enjoyed half a century at peace with itself. The army was abolished in 1948, and since then the country has practiced studied neutrality while turmoil raged around it. For an increasing number of visitors, Costa Rica offers an unbeatable combination of unfettered

Lake Atitlán

rainforest, dramatic scenery and, on the Pacific coast, some superb beaches.

Don't miss

San José, the capital, an excellent introduction to Central America for new visitors. A mile above sea level in the Central Valley of Costa Rica, it is a vibrant mix of earthiness and chic. The Museo de Oro Precolombino Oro contains a rich collection of pre-Columbian treasures, mined, refined and crafted by the indigenous people is also its most beautiful: forest populated with monkeys and exotic birds, beside three perfect beaches. Adjacent is the quietly prosperous port of Quepos.

Arenal, the perpetually smoldering volcano that presides over the west of the country. Even when shrouded in fog (as it often is), the steaming waters that flow down its perfectly conical sides are channeled into stylish spa resorts where you can rejuvenate weary limbs.

Monteverde Cloud Forest Biological Reserve, a project begun in the 1950s when a group of North American Quakers settled to the

Arenal

long before Columbus arrived at what he named the "rich coast." The nearby Teatro Nacional is a study in turn-of-the-century glamour.

Manuel Antonio National Park, on the Pacific Coast close to San José. Costa Rica's smallest protected area south of the Arenal volcano. They formed an agricultural collective, which still produces cheese, but have earmarked much of the surrounding land for preservation. There is a network of trails allowing the visitor excellent access to the

extraordinary variety of flora and fauna in Costa Rica.
Braulio Carrillo National Park, in the heart of the country, full of jagged canyons draped with virgin forest. A deftly constructed cable car enables you to glide across the rainforest at treetop level.

Cuba

Ever since Columbus first landed in 1492, Cuba has had an extraordinary history. Though the island is as large as the rest of the Antilles put together, the absence of mineral wealth meant it developed more slowly than the other Spanish colonies. Once the sugar trade became established, Cuba developed rapidly. Independence from Spain was achieved only a century ago, and until 1959 the country was run almost as a colony of the United States. Fidel Castro's revolution antagonized the US, so the Cuban leader turned to Moscow for support. This collapsed in 1991, causing a calamitous economic downturn. Recovery is dependent upon tourism, but US Treasury rules prevent Americans from taking vacations on the island.

Don't miss

Havana, the biggest city in the Caribbean and arguably the most beautiful. Habana Vieja, the old part of the city, is on the Unesco World Heritage list. Its elegant mansions ranged around handsome plazas are slowly being restored. In sharp contrast, the shoreline suburb of Miramar shows how the other half lived before the revolution.
Varadero, a twelve-mile stretch of silky white sand, and Cuba's leading beach resort – no longer the private preserve of US millionaires, it is becoming more and more like a European beach resort.
Santa Clara, scene of the decisive battle in the Revolution, led by Che Guevara – and, since 1997, final resting place of the world's most famous revolutionary.
Trinidad, another Unesco treasure, at the foot of the Sierra Escambray mountains. Much of the early 19th-century glory – colonial town-houses, wrought-iron street lamps that illuminate a maze of cobbled lanes – remains intact.
Santiago de Cuba, Cuba's second city, a more concise version of Havana with a pulse of its own. Much of the best Cuban music originates here. Santiago is also called the "Hero City of the Revolution," and contains the Moncada Barracks where Castro launched his first attack on the Batista regime. The date, July 26, 1953, is the holiest in the revolutionary calendar.
Baracoa, the first town to be established by the Spanish. This sleepy port is steeped in history, and is surrounded by fine scenery, including the magnificent plateau of El Yunque, the anvil-shaped mountain that dominates every view.

Holidays, festivals and events

Grim Reaper

January New Year (*Año Nuevo*) is celebrated widely and wildly throughout Latin America, especially Mexico, with considerable excitement, firecrackers, etc., in the capital. If you are planning to travel within Mexico at this time, note that bookings are likely to be extremely heavy. Epiphany (January 6) is also a public holiday, and the day when most Mexican children get their presents.

February Candlemas, on February 2, is the next big event, with plenty of processions. Depending on the year, late February may also be when Carnival takes place. The week leading up to the start of Lent is celebrated with verve, culminating in parades and fireworks on Mardi Gras (Shrove Tuesday).

Easter *Semana Santa*, Holy Week, takes place in March or April. The celebrations start on Palm Sunday, with most of the country closing down on Good Friday (*Viernes Santo*) for the Easter weekend. A very busy time to try to travel.

May Labor Day (*Día del Trabajo*) on May 1 is a public holiday, though without big celebrations. The same applies to May 5, *Cinco de Mayo*, the day in 1862 when the Mexicans beat the French at the battle of Puebla. Mothers' Day, May 10, is a fixed holiday too, the last for a few months. Corpus Christi (*Corpus Christi*) is sometimes celebrated in May, sometimes in June.

Día de los Meurtos

HOLIDAYS, FESTIVALS AND EVENTS

November The first two days of the month are spectacularly vibrant. All Saints' Day (*Todos los Santos*) on November 1 is a public holiday, and although it is used to commemorate dead children, is a happy event. The following day, All Souls, is the Day of the Dead (*Día de los Muertos*), when all-day parties are held in graveyards. This is an extremely exciting time to be in Mexico, or in Central America.

September Independence is celebrated with vigor on September 15 and 16, marking the call to arms in the war of independence against the Spanish.

October Columbus Day (October 12) is known as the *Día de la Raza* and marks the explorer's first landfall in the New World – actually in the Bahamas, a thousand miles from Mexico.

December Christmas (*Navidad*) is celebrated in the early hours of December 25, after midnight mass. Presents are saved until Epiphany.

If a holiday falls a day away from the weekend, on a Thursday or on a Tuesday, it is customary not to work on the Friday or Monday that is in the middle. This habit is referred to as *haciendo puente* (making a bridge), and people will say *Es puente* to explain why a shop is closed.

Bare necessities

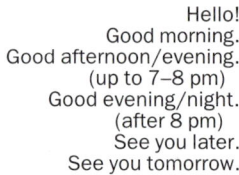

Greetings

Hello!	**¡Hola!**
Good morning.	**Buenos días.**
Good afternoon/evening. (up to 7–8 pm)	**Buenas tardes.**
Good evening/night. (after 8 pm)	**Buenas noches.**
See you later.	**Hasta luego/ Nos vemos.**
See you tomorrow.	**Hasta mañana/Nos vemos mañana.**
See you on Monday.	**Hasta el lunes/Nos vemos el lunes.**
Bye.	**Adiós.**
How are you?	**¿Cómo está?**
(Muy) bien, gracias, ¿y usted?	(Very) well, thank you, and you?

Other useful words

Please.	**Por favor.**
Thank you (very much).	**(Muchas) gracias.**
You're welcome.	**De nada.**
Excuse me.	**Con permiso.**
Sorry.	**Perdón /Perdone.**
Have a good day/time!	**¡Que le vaya bien!**
Have a good trip!	**¡Buen viaje!**
Have a nice meal!	**¡Buen provecho!**
Cheers!	**¡Salud!**
Here you are.	**Aquí tiene.**
OK.	**Bueno.**
It doesn't matter.	**No importa.**
Of course!	**¡Claro!**
yes/no	**sí/no**
sir/madam/miss	**señor/señora/señorita**
Can I (come in)?	**¿Se puede pasar?**
Let me introduce you to . . .	**Le presento a . . .**
Pleased to meet you.	**Mucho gusto.**
My pleasure.	**El gusto es mío.**

BARE NECESSITIES

Is/Are there . . . ?

Is there an elevator?	**¿Hay elevador?**
Are there any restrooms?	**¿Hay baños?**

Where is/are . . . ?

Where is the main square?	**¿Dónde está el Zócalo*?**
Where are the shops?	**¿Dónde están las tiendas?**
(It's/They are) on the right.	**(Está/están) a la derecha.**
(It's/They are) on the left.	**(Está/están) a la izquierda.**
* Peru, Argentina	**la Plaza de Armas**
Central America, Caribbean	**el Parque Central, la Plaza Mayor**

Do you have . . . ?

Do you have a room?	**¿Tiene un cuarto?**
Do you have any (unleaded gasoline/shrimps)?	**¿Tiene (gasolina sin plomo/ camarones)?**

How much . . . ?

How much does it cost?	**¿Cuánto cuesta?**
How much is (half a kilo/ a kilo) of tomatoes?	**¿Cuánto cuesta (medio kilo/un kilo) de jitomates?**
How much do they cost?	**¿Cuánto cuestan?**
How much are (the earrings)?	**¿Cuánto cuestan (los aretes)?**
How much is that (altogether)?	**¿Cuánto es?**

I'd like . . .

I'd like to see (the shirts).	**Quisiera ver (las camisas).**
I'd like a kilo of (oranges).	**¿Me da un kilo de (naranjas)?**

Getting things straight

Pardon?	**¿Cómo?**
Could you say that again, please?	**¿Puede repetir, por favor?**
More slowly, please.	**Más despacio, por favor.**
How do you spell it?	**¿Cómo se escribe?**
Will you write it for me, please?	**¿Me lo escribe, por favor?**
Is that right/Really?	**¿De verdad?**

BARE NECESSITIES

About yourself

My name is . . . , and you are . . . ?	**Me llamo . . . , ¿y usted?**
I'm from . . . , and you?	**Soy de . . . , ¿y usted?**
I live in . . .	**Vivo en . . .**
I'm a teacher.	**Soy maestro/a.***
I'm American.	**Soy americano** (man)/**americana** (woman)**.**
I speak a little Spanish.	**Hablo un poco de español.**
Do you speak English?	**¿Habla inglés?**

* The **o** ending is for males, the **a** is for females (see Language Builder p108).

Money

I'd like to change . . .	**Quisiera cambiar . . .**
traveler's checks	**cheques de viajero**
What is the dollar at?	**¿A cómo está el dólar?**
¿Tiene su pasaporte, por favor?	Can I see your passport, please?
El dólar está a ocho pesos.	The dollar is at 8 pesos.

What time?

What time is it?	**¿Qué hora es?**
at nine thirty	**a las nueve y media**
It's one o'clock.	**Es la una (en punto).**
It's (two/seven) o'clock.	**Son las (dos/siete) (en punto).**
It's (noon/midnight).	**Es (mediodía/medianoche).**
It's five past one.	**Es la una y cinco.**
It's ten past two.	**Son las dos y diez.**
It's a quarter past five.	**Son las cinco y cuarto.**
It's (twenty/twenty-five) past seven.	**Son las siete y (veinte/veinticinco).**
It's half past (eleven).	**Son las (once) y media.**
It's (twenty/twenty-five) to twelve.	**Son (veinte/veinticinco) para las doce.**
It's a quarter to eight.	**Son cuarto para las ocho.**
It's (ten/five) to six.	**Son (diez/cinco) para las seis.**
It's five to one.	**Son cinco para la una.**
. . . in the morning	**. . . de la mañana**
. . . in the afternoon/evening	**. . . de la tarde**
. . . in the evening/night	**. . . de la noche**

Numbers

0	cero	61	sesenta y uno/a
1	uno/a	70	setenta
2	dos	71	setenta y uno/a
3	tres	80	ochenta
4	cuatro	81	ochenta y uno/a
5	cinco	90	noventa
6	seis	91	noventa y uno/a
7	siete	100	cien
8	ocho	101	ciento uno/a
9	nueve	110	ciento diez
10	diez	120	ciento veinte
11	once	130	ciento treinta
12	doce	200	doscientos/as
13	trece	300	trescientos/as
14	catorce	420	cuatrocientos veinte
15	quince		
16	dieciséis	539	quinientos treinta y nueve
17	diecisiete		
18	dieciocho	648	seiscientos cuarenta y ocho
19	diecinueve		
20	veinte		
21	veintiuno/a	757	setecientos cincuenta y siete
22	veintidós		
23	veintitrés		
24	veinticuatro	866	ochocientos sesenta y seis
25	veinticinco		
26	veintiséis	975	novecientos setenta y cinco
27	veintisiete		
28	veintiocho		
29	veintinueve	1.000	mil
30	treinta	1.100	mil cien
31	treinta y uno/a	1.284	mil doscientos ochenta y cuatro
32	treinta y dos		
40	cuarenta		
41	cuarenta y uno/a	5.000	cinco mil
50	cinquenta		
51	cincuenta y uno/a	10.000	diez mil
		1.000.000	un millón
60	sesenta		

Ordinal numbers

1st	**primero**	5th	**quinto**	8th	**octavo**
2nd	**segundo**	6th	**sexto**	9th	**noveno**
3rd	**tercero**	7th	**séptimo**	10th	**décimo**
4th	**cuarto**				

Countries and nationalities

America	**América / Norteamérica: americano/a / norteamericano/a**
Argentina	**Argentina: argentino/a**
Australia	**Australia: australiano/a**
Austria	**Austria: austriaco/a**
Belgium	**Bélgica: belga**
Brasil	**Brasil: brasileño/a**
Canada	**Canadá: canadiense**
Chile	**Chile: chileno/a**
China	**China: chino/a**
Costa Rica	**Costa Rica: costarricense**
Cuba	**Cuba: cubano/a**
Denmark	**Dinamarca: dinamarqués/esa**
England	**Inglaterra: inglés/esa**
France	**Francia: francés/esa**
Germany	**Alemania: alemán/a**
Greece	**Grecia: griego/a**
Guatemala	**Guatemala: guatemalteco/a**
Honduras	**Honduras: hondureño/a**
India	**India: hindú**
Ireland	**Irlanda: irlandés/esa**
Italy	**Italia: italiano/a**
Japan	**Japón: japonés/esa**
Mexico	**México: mexicano/a**
Netherlands	**Países Bajos / Holanda: holandés/esa**
New Zealand	**Nueva Zelanda: neocelandés/esa**
Northern Ireland	**Irlanda del Norte: irlandés/a**
Norway	**Noruega: noruego/a**
Peru	**Perú: peruano/a**
Portugal	**Portugal: portugués/esa**
Russia	**Rusia: ruso/a**
Scotland	**Escocia: escocés/esa**
South Africa	**Sudáfrica / Suráfrica: sudafricano/a / surafricano/a**
Spain	**España: español/a**
Sweden	**Suecia: sueco/a**
United States	**Estados Unidos: estadounidense/ norteamericano/ a**

BARE NECESSITIES

Colors

beige	**beige**	pink	**rosa**
black	**negro/a**	red	**rojo/a**
blue	**azul**	white	**blanco/a**
brown	**café**	yellow	**amarillo/a**

Days of the week

What day is it today? **¿Qué día es hoy?**

Sunday	**domingo**	Thursday	**jueves**
Monday	**lunes**	Friday	**viernes**
Tuesday	**martes**	Saturday	**sábado**
Wednesday	**miércoles**		

today/yesterday/tomorrow	**hoy/ayer/mañana**
the day after tomorrow	**pasado mañana**
tonight	**hoy en la noche**
last night	**anoche**
this Saturday	**el sábado/este sábado**
next (Monday/week)	**(el lunes/la semana) que viene**
last (Sunday)	**(el domingo) pasado**
(at) the weekend	**el fin de semana**

Months

(on) March 26th	**el veintiséis de marzo**
What month is carnival?	**¿En qué mes es el carnaval?**
At the beginning of . . .	**A principios de . . .**
In the middle of . . .	**A mediados de . . .**
At the end of . . .	**A fines de . . .**

January	**enero**	July	**julio**
February	**febrero**	August	**agosto**
March	**marzo**	September	**septiembre**
April	**abril**	October	**octubre**
May	**mayo**	November	**noviembre**
June	**junio**	December	**diciembre**

The seasons

spring	**la primavera**
autumn	**el otoño**
summer	**el verano**
winter	**el invierno**

Sound check

There are only five vowel sounds in Spanish, one for each vowel.

a	like **a** in *father*	**casa**	*kahsa*
		nada	*nahdah*
e	like **e** in *Ben*	**tele**	*tehleh*
		en	*ehn*
i	like **ee** in *been*	**mira**	*meerah*
		kilo	*keeloa*
o	like **o** in *nod*	**por favor**	*poar fahvoar*
u	like **oo** in *food*	**mucho gusto**	*moochoa goostoa*

Language works

A refreshing pause

1 You and your friend decide to get a cup of coffee in a cafeteria
- □ **Buenas tardes, señores.**
- ■ **Buenas tardes. ¿Tiene capuchino?**
- □ **Sí, claro.**
- ■ **Dos capuchinos, por favor.**
- □ **Sí, señor.**

- ■ **¿Cuánto es?**
- □ **Son trece pesos.**

How much were the cappuccinos?

Money matters

2 You walk into a Casa de Cambio to change money
- □ **Buenos días.**
- ■ **Buenos días ¿A cómo está el dólar?**
- □ **Está a . . . ocho pesos.**
- ■ **Bueno. Quisiera cambiar cheques de viajero, cien dólares.**
- □ **Sí señor. ¿Tiene su pasaporte, por favor?**
- ■ **Aquí tiene.**

Roughly how many pesos will you get for your money?
What did the assistant ask you for?

Making friends

3 At the hotel reception, you run into an Argentinian guest you had briefly met the day before
- □ **¡Hola! Buenos días.**
- ■ **Buenos días. ¿Cómo está?**
- □ **Muy bien, y usted?**
- ■ **Bien, gracias.**
- □ **Bueno, adiós. ¡Que le vaya bien!**

What did the Argentinian wish you?

BARE NECESSITIES

Try it out

Missing vowels

What are the missing vowels in these numbers?
ctr ch dz dcss vnt
cncnt nvnt cn trscnts
ml

Get it right

What do you say when you . . .
1 need to go to the restroom in a museum?
2 greet somebody after 8 pm?
3 are about to have a drink?
4 want to get past somebody blocking your way?
5 want to know the price of some earrings?
6 are going to the fifth floor and don't want to use the stairs?
7 have accidentally stepped on someone's foot?

As if you were there

You start talking to a Mexican during your flight to Cancún
☐ **¿Va a Cancún?**
■ (Ask him to speak more slowly)
☐ **Cancún. ¿Va a Cancún?**
■ (Say yes)
☐ **¿Es americano/a?**
■ (Say your nationality and the name of your home town)
☐ **Soy del DF**
■ (Say "Pardon?")
☐ **Del DF . . . de la Ciudad de México, pero vivo en Cancún. Me llamo Andrés. Andrés Parra, ¿y usted?**
■ (Say you are pleased to meet him and tell him your name)
☐ **El gusto es mío.**

Getting around

Car and taxi

Car rental is relatively inexpensive in Mexico, and the highway system is mostly in good condition. Unless you are confident in your ability to drive defensively among some of the world's more imaginative motorists, though, you may prefer to let someone else do the driving. Taking a taxi through Mexico City is a good way to decide if you will enjoy it (see p8 for more details). Most taxi drivers don't expect a tip (although it is fairly common to round the fare up), but US-sized tips of around 15% are on the increase in tourist centers such as Cancún and Puerto Vallarta.

> I'd like to rent a car.
> **Quisiera alquilar un coche.**

The nation's roads were substantially upgraded in the 1970s and 1980s, and now it is possible to drive the length or breadth of Mexico on good, well-surfaced highways – most of them free of tolls. Things get trickier in towns and cities, and in remote rural areas, where potholes are frequent and driver behavior particularly erratic.

One useful feature of driving in Mexico is the fleet of *Angeles Verdes* (Green Angels), English-speaking mechanics who patrol main highways and make repairs for free (though you pay for any gas or parts).

Gas stations on main routes are frequent, selling both leaded and unleaded fuel, but if you are planning to stray far from the beaten track, then take advice and spare fuel.

Finally, be warned that in parts of Mexico at high altitude, snow and ice can be a hazard.

Buses

Most Mexicans rely on the country's fast, frequent and economical long-distance bus network. On main routes, such as Mexico City to Guadalajara or Mérida to Cancún, there can be four or more departures every hour. Most cities have large, modern bus stations (*central de autobuses* or *terminal*), with competing companies offering services on most routes, thereby keeping prices low.

> Are there buses to Cancún?
> **¿Hay autobuses para Cancún?**

A couple of drawbacks: bus stations tend to be treated as other countries treat airports, ie keeping them well away from the center of town. The terminus is often a taxi or local bus ride away. And you cannot rely on getting impartial information from competing operators. If you ask for the time of the next bus to Veracruz, a bus company official will probably tell you the time of departure for his or her fleet (even if a rival's leaves much earlier).

GETTING AROUND

Finding space on a particular bus is not usually a problem, except on Friday and Sunday evenings and around festival times. Many bus companies have computerized ticketing and reservation systems that can book you a seat on any service in a few seconds; "unbooking," or changing a reservation, is likely to be slow and/or expensive, so try not to book until you are sure you know when you want to travel.

On board, you can expect heavy air-conditioning and noisy videos. The local people seem to have a knack of sleeping soundly through these, which is something foreigners cannot usually manage. On longer journeys, rest stops are made every few hours at road houses where the refreshment facilities are generally good.

Train

Mexico's rail service has fallen into such abject disrepair that there is only one service worth recommending: the Chihuahua al Pacífico route, popularly known as the Copper Canyon Railway. This operates with ramshackle old rolling stock and is often many hours late, but it is also one of the world's great railway journeys. The line runs daily between Chihuahua and Los Mochis, close to the Pacific Coast, and provides the only direct surface link between the two regions. It winds through spectacular mountain forests, and pauses for ten minutes to allow passengers to look down into the vast chasm of the Copper Canyon. It should be on every traveler's itinerary. Elsewhere, stick to the buses or planes.

> Where is the ticket office?
> **¿Dónde está la taquilla?**

Air

Given the size of Mexico, flying is the obvious form of transportation for visitors who wish to see a lot of the country within a short time. For decades, Mexico has had two heavily controlled airlines, Aeroméxico and Mexicana. Both have tended to operate on the same routes at the same times. Now, though, aviation liberalization as found in the US and Europe has caught on. More airlines are being allowed to fly, and the quality of in-flight service has improved.

The best deals are available to visitors who book in advance and take advantage of the air passes offered by the main airlines; typically, these divide the country into a number of zones and offer fares within and between these zones for significantly less than the normal fares. But even if you wait until you arrive in Mexico and buy tickets on an ad-hoc basis, you will find that fares compare favorably with those charged in most other countries. Most Mexican travel agents are well-informed about available services.

Sea

The only significant ferry operations are those linking ports on the eastern side of Baja California with the trunk of Mexico.

GETTING AROUND

Phrasemaker

Asking the way

Excuse me	**Perdone**
Is there a (bank/pharmacy) near here?	**¿Hay (un banco/una farmacia) por aquí?**
Where is the (market/beach), please?	**¿Dónde está (el mercado/la playa), por favor?**

No (no hay).	No (there isn't one).
Allí está.	There it is.
a (una cuadra/dos cuadras)	(one block/two blocks) away
(aquí) derecho	straight ahead
en la (primera/segunda) a la (derecha/izquierda)	on the (first/second) on the (left/right)
en la esquina (de la Calle X y la Calle Y)	on the corner (of X and Y streets)
a cien metros	100 meters away
al final de la calle	at the end of the street
(bastante) lejos	(quite) far
junto (al banco/a la iglesia)	next to the (bank/church)
enfrente (del museo/de la catedral)	in front of/opposite (the museum/the cathedral)
detrás (del hotel/de la tienda)	behind (the hotel/the shop)

speed bumps

GETTING AROUND

Places to look for

beach	**la playa**
bureau de change	**una casa de cambio**
bus station	**la terminal de autobuses**
bus stop	**una parada (de autobuses/de camiones*)**
cathedral	**la catedral**
change	**cambio**
church	**la iglesia/el templo**
gas station	**una gasolinera**
main square	**el Zócalo†**
market	**el mercado**

museum	**el museo**
palace	**el palacio**
park	**el parque**
pharmacy	**una farmacia**
Post Office	**el Correo**
pyramids	**las pirámides**
restaurant	**un restaurante**
restroom	**el baño**
ruins	**las ruinas**
(handicrafts) shop	**una tienda (de artesanías)**
street	**la calle**
swimming pool	**la alberca**
Tourist Information Office	**la Oficina de Turismo**
town center	**el centro**
Town Hall	**la Presidencia Municipal**
* Caribbean	**una parada de guaguas**
† Caribbean, Central America	**la Plaza Mayor/el Parque Central**

GETTING AROUND

Renting a car or bike

a rental car	**un coche* de alquiler**
a small car	**un coche chico**
a (fairly) big car	**un coche (bastante) grande**
I'd like to rent a (car/bicycle).	**Quisiera alquilar (un coche/una bicicleta).**
for (three days/a week)	**por (tres días/una semana)**
How much is it per (day/week)?	**¿Cuánto cuesta por (día/semana)?**
Is (insurance/mileage/tax) included?	**¿Está incluido el (seguro/kilometraje/IVA)?**
Is the insurance comprehensive?	**¿El seguro es contra todo riesgo?**
Do I have to pay a deposit?	**¿Tengo que pagar depósito?**

* some parts of Latin America   **carro**

CURVA PELIGROSA A 500 m

(See p33 for numbers.)

¿Qué tipo?	What type?
¿Por cuánto tiempo?	For how long?
Tenemos . . .	We have . . .
quinientos pesos al día	five hundred pesos a day
dos mil pesos a la semana	Two thousand pesos a week
Es aparte.	It's extra.
Su licencia*, por favor.	Your driver's license, please.
Tenemos (choferes/guías) que hablan inglés.	We have English-speaking (drivers/guides).

* Peru/Argentina   **brevete/registro**

Some road signs

Camino en reparación	Road construction
Conserve su derecha	Keep right
Cuidado con el (ganado/tren)	Watch out for (cattle/trains)
Curva peligrosa	Dangerous curve
Despacio	(Go) slowly
Disminuya su velocidad	Slow down
México cuota	Mexico (City) via toll road
México libre	Mexico (City) via free road
No hay paso	No entry
Peligro	Danger
Topes	Speed bumps
Tramo en construcción	Road construction
Tramo en reparación	Road repairs
Un solo carril a 100 metros	One lane only 100m ahead
Zona de derrumbes	Falling rock area

GETTING AROUND

Getting petrol

gasoline	**la gasolina***
30 litres of unleaded gas	**treinta litros de gasolina* sin plomo**
Fill it up, please.	**Lleno, por favor.**
Please check the (oil/water/tires).	**Por favor revise (el aceite/el agua/las llantas†).**
Here's the key.	**Tenga la llave.**

¿Le reviso (el aceite/el agua/las llantas†)?	Shall I check your (oil/water/tires)?
(Está/Están) bien.	(It's/They're) OK.
Le falta (aceite/agua/aire).	You need (oil/water/air).

* South America	**la bencina/la nafta**
† Argentina	**las ruedas**

Finding the way

Is the road to Coba in good condition?	**¿Está buena la carretera a Cobá?**
Is this the road to Palenque?	**¿Es ésta la carretera a Palenque?**
Do you have to pay a toll?	**¿Hay que pagar cuota?**
Is Chichen Itza far?	**¿Está lejos Chichén Itzá?**
How far is Taxco?	**¿Qué tan lejos está Taxco?**

No, es brecha.	No, it's a dirt road.
Sí, hay caseta(s) de cobro.	Yes, there (is/are) (a) toll booth(s).
Está (como) a treinta kilómetros.	It's (about) 30 kilometers away.

GETTING AROUND

Using the subway

the subway	**el metro***
A ticket, please.	**Un boleto, por favor.**
Does this train go to Bellas Artes?	**¿Este tren va a Bellas Artes?**
What line is Universidad on?	**¿En qué línea está Universidad?**
Where do I change for Zócalo?	**¿Dónde cambio para Zócalo?**
Is the next station Hidalgo?	**¿La próxima estación es Hidalgo?**
Does this train end up at Observatorio?	**¿Este tren va en dirección Observatorio?**
* Argentina	**el subte**

en la línea dos	on line 2
Tome la línea dos (dirección Tasqueña).	Take line 2 (going towards Tasqueña).
Cambie en Pino Suárez.	Change at Pino Suárez.

Catching a taxi or (mini)bus

Is there a taxi stand?
¿Hay un sitio de taxis?

To the (airport/cathedral), please.
(Al aeropuerto/a la catedral), por favor.

Is there a mini-bus stop (near here)?
¿Hay una parada de colectivos por aquí?

Where can I get a bus?	**¿Dónde puedo tomar (un camión/un autobús*)?**
Do you go past the Poliforum Siqueiros?	**¿Pasa por el Poliforum Siqueiros?**
How much is it (to the San Angel Inn restaurant)?	**¿Cuánto es (al restaurante San Angel Inn)?**
Is it far?	**¿Está lejos?**
Can you tell me where to get off?	**¿Me dice dónde bajarme?**
Keep the change.	**Quédese con el cambio.**
Could I have a receipt?	**¿Me da un recibo?**
* Caribbean	**una guagua**

A media hora, más o menos.	About half an hour.
Aquí es.	It's here.

GETTING AROUND

Trains, buses and planes

Are there (buses/trains/planes) to . . . ?	¿Hay (autobuses/trenes/aviones) para . . . ?
What time does the (bus/train/plane) to Querétaro leave?	¿A qué hora sale el (autobús/tren/avión) para Querétaro?
What time does it arrive?	¿A qué hora llega?
Which (platform/gate) does it leave from?	¿De qué (andén/puerta) sale?
How long does it take?	¿Cuánto tarda?
Is it air conditioned?	¿Tiene aire acondicionado?
Does it have a restroom?	¿Tiene baño?
Do you have a schedule?	¿Tiene un horario?

Salen cada hora. They leave every hour.
Tarda (seis) horas. It takes (six) hours.
(See p32 for time)

Booking and buying a ticket

Where is the ticket office?	**¿Dónde está la taquilla?**
A one-way ticket, please.	**Un boleto de ida, por favor.**
a round-trip ticket	**un boleto de ida y vuelta**
two adults and one child	**dos adultos y un niño**
smoking/non-smoking	**fumar/no fumar**
I'd like to reserve (a seat/a berth).	**Quisiera reservar (un asiento/una alcoba).**

Monte Albán, Oaxaca

Sound check

In Spanish, the vowels always represent the same sound, whatever their position in words. Even in diphthongs – when two vowels occur together in one syllable – they keep their individual original sounds.

bueno *booehnoa*
gracias *grahseeahs*
tienda *teeendah*

h is always silent . . .
hay *aee* **hola** *oalah*

. . . except in the combination **ch**
chocolate *chokolahteh*

Practice saying these words:
**hora   tiene   restaurante
hoy   anoche   autobús
vuelta   aire   hay   buen viaje**

Language works

Asking the way

1 You ask a passerby for help
■ **¿Perdone, dónde está el Museo Frida Kahlo?**
□ **Derecho, a dos cuadras. En la esquina de Allende y Londres.**

Is the Frida Kahlo Museum far?

Renting a car

2 Inquiring about car rental
■ **Quisiera alquilar un coche chico.**
□ **Tenemos un VW Sedán.**
■ **¿Cuánto cuesta por semana?**
□ **Dos mil pesos, con seguro incluido.**
■ **¿Es contra todo riesgo?**
□ **Sí.**
(**con** = with)

How much is it to rent a VW Beetle for a week?

Getting gas

3 You get service from the gas station attendant
■ **Lleno, por favor.**
□ **Muy bien . . .**
■ **Y revise las llantas, por favor. Dieciocho y veintitrés.**

□ **¿Le reviso el aceite?**
■ **No, gracias. Está bien.**

What does the gas station attendant offer to do?

Finding the way

4 You would like to drive to Puerto Escondido
■ **¿Está buena la carretera a Puerto Escondido?**
□ **Sí, muy buena.**
■ **¿Está lejos Puerto Escondido?**
□ **No, como a ciento cincuenta kilómetros.**

Puerto Escondido is a hundred and fifty kilometers away and the road is very good: true/false?

GETTING AROUND

Using the subway

5 You are at Hidalgo subway station checking you have the right train
- ¿Este tren va a Bellas Artes?
- □ No, para Bellas Artes tome la línea dos, dirección Tasqueña.
- Gracias.

Which line do you need to take?

road construction

A good way to travel

6 You are thinking of taking a bus to Acapulco
- ¿A qué horas hay autobuses para Acapulco?
- □ El de lujo sale cada hora, a la media.
- ¿Cuánto tarda?
- □ Seis horas.
- Dos boletos, para las dos y media.

(**el de lujo** = the luxury one)

How frequent are the buses for Acapulco?
How long does the trip take?

Try it out

Find the right place

Where do you go to:
1 send your postcards home?
2 buy handicrafts?
3 take a bus to another city?
4 get aspirin?
5 get information on tourist attractions?
6 swim?
7 get gas?

Mix and match

Match the questions (1–5) and the answers (a–e).

1 ¿Perdone, hay un restaurante por aquí?
2 ¿Dónde está el Correo, por favor?
3 ¿Cuánto cuesta?
4 ¿Cuánto tarda?
5 Quisiera alquilar un coche.

a Seis o siete horas.
b Cuatrocientos pesos al día.
c ¿Para cuánto tiempo?
d Allí en la esquina.
e Sí, hay dos o tres al final de la calle.

As if you were there

You stop a minibus
- (Ask if it goes past Bellas Artes)
- □ Sí, enfrente.
- (Ask how much it is to Bellas Artes)
- □ Diez pesos por persona.
- (You hand the driver the money and ask him to tell you where to get off)
- □ Sí, no está lejos.

- □ Aquí es. (pointing) Allí está Bellas Artes.
- (Thank him)

Somewhere to stay

At a glance

■ Tourist offices can provide lists of accommodation and offer advice on particular places to stay.
■ Even if you have no reservation, and the tourist office is closed, in most towns at most times of the year you can find a room with little difficulty.
■ At festival times you should consider booking in advance.

Types of accommodation

Most visitors stay in hotels, though for travelers on a budget there are low-cost alternatives such as *casas de huéspedes* (guest houses, simple and inexpensive) and *villas juveniles* (youth hostels). At beach areas there are two further alternatives: *cabañas* (simple huts usually equipped with a hammock) and camping – all beaches are considered public property, where it is permissable to pitch a tent; few foreign visitors take the safety risk, however. If you do want to camp, there is a growing number of campsites with excellent facilities.

Hotels

The usual star ratings apply to Mexican hotels, which range from cheap and shabby properties to the most lavish luxury hotels – but while the former can be found all over Mexico, the latter are concentrated in the largest cities and resort areas. Many visitors find the most appealing hotels are those housed in former private mansions. In provincial towns, these are often known as *posadas*.

🔔 Do you have a room?
¿Tiene una habitación libre?

As in the United States, the price of a room does not normally include breakfast. Conversely, an increasing number of hotels are becoming "all-inclusive," providing foreign visitors with unlimited food and drink.

Rentals

The concept of rental apartments is catching on in coastal areas, but is mostly restricted to certain types of package vacations and to timeshare properties. There is normally a convenient supermarket, though prices may be high.

Phrasemaker

Places to stay

un camping	campsite
un departamento/apartamento rentado	apartment to let
una hacienda	old ranch converted into a first-class hotel or restaurant
un hotel	hotel
una villa juvenil	youth hostel
un motel	motel
una pensión/una casa de huéspedes	boardinghouse
una posada	mansion converted into a hotel

Finding a place

Do you have a room?	**¿Tiene una habitación* libre?**
a (single/double) room	**una habitación (individual/doble)**
for three people	**para tres personas**
for two nights	**para dos noches**
with a bathroom	**con baño**
Can I see the room?	**¿Puedo ver la habitación*?**
How much is the room?	**¿Cuánto cuesta la habitación*?**
Do you have anything cheaper?	**¿Tiene algo más barato?**
We'll think about it.	**Vamos a pensarlo.**
We'll take it.	**Está bien.**
* Mexico (informal)	**un cuarto**
¿Para cuántas noches?	For how many nights?
¿Para cuántas personas?	For how many people?
Perdone.	I'm sorry.
Está todo lleno.	We're full.
Los niños pagan la mitad.	Children pay half price.
Para servirle.	You're welcome (literally "At your service").

Specifications

Does it have (a bathroom/a shower/an ocean view)?	¿Tiene (baño/ducha/vista al mar)?
with a double bed	con cama matrimonial
with twin beds	con dos camas
Is (breakfast/tax) included?	¿Está incluido (el desayuno/el impuesto (el IVA))?
How much is it with meals?	¿Cuánto cuesta con comidas?
How much is it without meals?	¿Cuánto cuesta sin comidas?
How much is an extra bed?	¿Cuánto cuesta una cama extra?

El desayuno es aparte.	(Breakfast/tax) is extra.
todo incluido	everthing included
No incluye comidas.	Meals are not included.
No tenemos camas matrimoniales.	We don't have any double beds.

Checking in and getting information

I have a reservation.	**Tengo una reservación.**
In the name of . . .	**A nombre de . . .**
for the 14th	**para el día 14**
What floor is it on?	**¿En qué piso está?**
Where's (the elevator/the staircase)?	**¿Dónde está (el elevador/la escalera)?**
What time is (breakfast/dinner)?	**¿A qué hora es (el desayuno/la cena)?**
Is there air conditioning?	**¿Hay aire acondicionado?**
Where can I park?	**¿Dónde me puedo estacionar?**

(Su nombre/Su pasaporte), por favor.	(Your name/Your passport), please.
¿Quiere llenar esta forma?	Please fill in this form.
(Es) la habitación número . . .	(It's) room number . . .
Está en el tercer piso.	It's on the third floor.

(See p33 for numbers.)

SOMEWHERE TO STAY

La escalera está a mano derecha.	The stairs are on the right.
El elevador está a mano izquierda.	The elevator is on the left.
de (las) siete a (las) diez y media	from seven to ten thirty
(See p32 for times.)	
Tenemos estacionamiento.	We have a parking lot.
¿Cuál es su número de placa?	Your license plate number?
¿Van a cenar?	Are you going to have dinner?
Aquí está la llave.	Here's the key.

Hotel staff

bellboy	**el botones**
chambermaid	**la recamarera**
manager	**(el/la) gerente**
receptionist	**(el/la) recepcionista**
switchboard operator	**(el/la) operador(a)**
waiter	**el mesero**
waitress	**la mesera**

Facilities

air conditioning	**aire acondicionado**
bar	**bar**
garden	**jardín**
hot water	**agua caliente**
laundry service	**servicio de lavandería**
minibar	**servibar**
restaurant	**restaurante**
room service	**servicio en el cuarto**
safe-deposit box	**caja fuerte**
sauna	**sauna**
swimming pool	**piscina/alberca**
telephone	**teléfono**
tennis court	**cancha de tennis**
TV	**televisión**

SOMEWHERE TO STAY

Problems

My room hasn't been made up.	**No me han hecho el cuarto.**
There (isn't a/aren't any) . . .	**No hay . . .**
How do you work . . . ?	**¿Cómo funciona . . .?**
. . . isn't working.	**. . . no funciona.**
(Ahora/Ahorita) le mando a alguien.	I'll send someone up right away.
Le mando (uno/una/unos/unas).	I'll send you (one/some).

In your room

blankets	**cobijas**	restroom/bathroom	**el baño/el excusado**
hangers	**ganchos**	shower	**la regadera/la ducha**
fan	**el ventilador**	soap	**jabón**
faucet	**la llave del agua**	telephone	**el teléfono**
lamp	**la lámpara**	toilet paper	**papel de baño**
light	**la luz**	towels	**toallas**
lock	**la cerradura**		
pillows	**almohadas**		

Asking for help

Could I have a wake-up call at . . . ?	**¿Me puede despertar a las . . .?**
Could you get me a taxi?	**¿Me puede conseguir un taxi?**
Could you send the bellboy up?	**¿Me puede mandar al botones?**
Do you have a map of the (town/area)?	**¿Tiene un mapa (de la ciudad/del área)?**
Do you sell stamps?	**¿Vende (estampillas/timbres)?**
Is there a mail box in the hotel?	**¿Hay buzón en el hotel?**

Checking out

I'd like to pay the bill. (by credit card/with traveler's checks/with cash)

Quiero pagar la cuenta. (con tarjeta de crédito/con cheques de viajero/en efectivo)

I think there's a mistake.

Creo que hay un error.

¿Qué habitación? Which room?
La llave, por favor. Your key, please.
¿Cómo va a pagar? How are you going to pay?
¡Buen viaje! Have a good trip!
¿Quiere firmar aquí? Sign here, please.
Aquí tiene su recibo. Here's your receipt.

Campsites

Do you have a space for (a tent/a camper)?

¿Tiene lugar para (una tienda/un trailer)?

How much is it per (person/tent/camper)?

¿Cuánto cuesta por (persona/tienda/trailer)?

Is there (a shop/a laundry/a swimming pool)?

¿Hay (tienda/lavandería/alberca)?

Where are (the showers/the trash cans/the restrooms)?

¿Dónde están (las regaderas/los basureros/los baños)?

Cuesta . . . pesos por (persona/coche/tienda/trailer).

It costs . . . pesos per (person/car/tent/camper).

Rentals

I'd like to rent (a villa/an apartment).

Quisiera rentar (una casa/un departamento).

How does the stove work?

¿Cómo funciona la estufa?

SOMEWHERE TO STAY

Sound check

Spanish word stress patterns are very consistent and follow two rules:

1 In words ending in a vowel or **n** or **s**, the stress falls on the second to the last syllable.
amigo   mañana   buenas

2 In words ending in a consonant other than **n** or **s**, the stress falls on the last syllable.
hotel   comer   pagar   ¡Salud!

When these rules are broken, the word has an acute accent ´; the stress then falls on the accented syllable, whatever the ending. The accent does not change the sound quality of the vowel where it falls.
difícil   menú   pensión

Practice on these words:
**ducha   elevador   reservación
está   teléfono   noches**

Language works

Finding a place to stay

1 You get a room
- ☐ **Buenas tardes.**
- ■ **Buenas tardes. ¿Tienen un cuarto libre?**
- ☐ **¿Individual o doble?**
- ■ **Doble.**
- ☐ **Sí tenemos. ¿Para cuántas noches?**
- ■ **Una noche.**
- ☐ **Muy bien.**
- ■ **¿Cuánto cuesta?**
- ☐ **Cuatrocientos pesos.**

How much is your double room?

Specifications

2 You check what is available in your double room
- ■ **¿Tiene baño el cuarto?**
- ☐ **Sí, claro. Todos los cuartos tienen baño.**
- ■ **Bien. Y ¿tiene cama matrimonial?**
- ☐ **No, son dos camas individuales.**
- ■ **¿No tiene con cama matrimonial?**
- ☐ **No, sólo con dos camas.**
- ■ **Bueno, está bien.**

(**sólo** = only)

You get a bathroom: true/false?
You'll be sleeping in a double bed: true/false?

Checking prices

3 Your reservation turns out OK
- ■ **Tengo una reservación a nombre de Westwood.**
- ☐ **Una reservación . . . Westwood . . . Sí, aquí está. Una habitación individual para dos noches.**
- ■ **¿Cuánto cuesta la habitación?**
- ☐ **Trescientos pesos la noche.**
- ■ **¿Está incluido el desayuno?**
- ☐ **No, el desayuno es aparte – cuesta cincuenta pesos.**
- ■ **Muy bien.**
- ☐ **Su pasaporte, por favor. Y, ¿quiere llenar esta forma?**

(**aquí está** = here it is)

SOMEWHERE TO STAY

How much will you pay for two nights and two breakfasts?
What two things do you have to do next?

Checking out

4 You check out and pay the bill
- Quiero pagar la cuenta.
- Sí, señor. ¿Qué habitación?
- Ochenta y nueve. ¿Cuánto es?
- Cuatrocientos sesenta y siete pesos, todo incluido. ¿Cómo va a pagar?
- Con tarjeta de crédito.
- Muy bien . . . ¿quiere firmar aquí? . . . Gracias. Aquí tiene su recibo. Adiós y buen viaje.

You pay less than five hundred pesos: true/false?
You got a receipt: true/false?

At the campsite

5 You have just arrived
- ¿Tienen lugar para una tienda?
- Sí, ¿para cuántas noches?
- Una noche. ¿Cuánto cuesta?
- Cien pesos.
- ¿Hay alberca?
- Sí, claro.

Is there a swimming pool?

Try it out

"A" puzzle

Only the letter **a** remains in these words. Use the definitions to complete them.

1 _ a _ _ _ a _ _ _ _
   A place to sleep
2 _ _ a _ _
   Necessary to get into your room
3 _ _ _ _ a _ _ _
   An easy way to get to the top floor
4 _ _ _ _ a _ _ a _ _ _
   Where you eat if you don't ask for room service
5 _ _ _ a _ _ _ _
   The first meal of the day

As if you were there

You pick up the phone in your room.
- Recepción, buenas noches.
- (Complain that there is no toilet paper)
- Perdone, ahorita le mando un rollo.
- (Thank him and ask for a wake-up call at 7)
- Sí, cómo no.

Buying things

Shops

Most stores open from 8 am or 9 am to 12 pm or 1 pm, and again from 4 pm to 7 pm or 8 pm, daily except

Sunday. Mexico city is the exception – most places forgo the siesta. In heavy tourist areas, too, shops may open all day, every day. Most stores accept credit cards – this is no longer a likely indicator of high prices. In tourist areas, many shops are happy to accept US dollars in cash or traveler's checks. Note, however, that the rate of exchange you get is likely to be considerably worse than it would be from a bank. All quoted prices should include sales tax (IVA).

! How much is it?
¿Cuánto cuesta?

Best-value goods

Textiles
Designs and materials of Indian origin are colorful, easy to find, and often extremely good value.
Leather
Prices for shoes, jackets, belts and handbags are usually much lower than north of the border.
Pottery
Anything from simple terracotta plant pots to intricately decorated plates, vases and tiles.

! What is it made of?
¿De qué está hecho/a?

BUYING THINGS

Jewelry
For gold, Oaxaca is the best place to look; for silver, try Taxco.
Hats and baskets
Woven baskets make excellent gifts, while a well-made hat can give useful protection against the sun during your visit.
Wine
Quality has increased so much in Mexico that taking home a few bottles can be worthwhile – but check your duty-free limits first.

Great markets

Every town has a regular market, always a colorful occasion. Prices for items that are clearly aimed at tourists are usually open to negotiation, but otherwise the price you see is the price you pay. These markets are recommended for buying snacks or souvenirs, or for their aesthetic value.

Mercado de la Merced, Mexico City Perhaps the biggest and busiest in the country, if not the whole of Latin America.
Museo de Artes e Industrias Populares, Chihuahua More of a market than the museum that the name suggests, particularly good for warm clothing – this is one of Mexico's cooler cities.
Mercado Hidalgo, Tijuana A good introduction for first-time visitors to Mexico.
Casa de las Artesanías, Monterrey Interesting examples of lead crystal, the local specialty.
Mercado Libertad, Guadalajara, a vast covered market with some excellent places to eat
Mercado Juárez and Mercado 20 de Noviembre, Oaxaca A matching pair of markets with a broad range of products and delicious food.

Buying food

Many visitors find the cost of eating out so modest that they never bother buying and preparing food themselves. Fixing up a picnic for a day outdoors is quick and easy, though. Supermarkets are catching on rapidly in Mexico, but most local people shop for food at markets. You can assemble the ingredients for a decent picnic easily and economically.

57

Phrasemaker

Phrases to use anywhere

What time do they (open/close)?	¿A qué hora (abren/cierran)?
Do you have any (corn oil/envelopes)?	¿Tiene (aceite de maíz/sobres)?
How much (is it/are they)?	¿Cuánto (cuesta/cuestan)?
How much are (the bananas/the plums)?	¿Cuánto cuestan (los plátanos/las ciruelas)?
I'll have (two kilos/a hundred grams), please.	Deme (dos kilos/cien gramos), por favor.
I prefer the other one.	Prefiero (el otro/la otra).*
this (one)	éste/ésta*
these (ones)	éstos/éstas
that (one)	ése/ésa
those (ones)	ésos/ésas
I'm just looking.	Sólo estoy mirando.
How much is it (altogether)?	¿Cuánto es?
Nothing else, thanks.	Nada más, gracias.
(It's/They're) very nice.	(Es/Son) muy bonito/a/os/as.
(It's/They're) (very) expensive.	(Es/Son) (muy) caro/a/os/as.
Is that your best price?	¿Es el último precio?
I'll give you fifty pesos.	Le doy cincuenta pesos.
Do you have anything cheaper?	¿Tiene algo más barato?

¿En qué puedo servirle?	Can I help you?
¿Qué desea?	What would you like?
¿Le (gusta/gustan)?	Do you like (it/them)?
¿(Cuánto/cuánta)* quiere?	How much would you like?
¿(Cuántos/cuántas)* quiere?	How many would you like?
Claro que sí.	Of course.
¿Qué más va a llevar?	What else would you like?
¿Algo más?	Anything else?
Perdone, no tenemos.	I'm sorry, we don't have any.
Sólo tengo . . .	I only have . . .
Aquí tiene.	Here you are.
Son quinientos cuarenta pesos.	That's 540 pesos.
Es precio fijo.	The price is fixed.

* To be more accurate with masculine/feminine endings, see p108.

BUYING THINGS

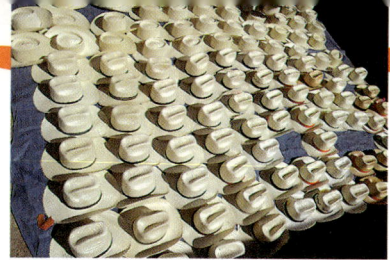

Where to shop

bakery	una panadería	market	un mercado, un tianguis (Mex)
barber	una peluquería		
bookstore	una librería		
butcher	una carnicería	newsstand	un puesto de periódicos
cake shop	una pastelería		
fruit store	una frutería	phamacy	una farmacia
general store	una miscelánea	produce store	una verdularia
jeweler	una joyería	shoe store	una zapatería
hairdresser	un salón de belleza	shopping center	un centro comercial
handicraft shop	una tienda de artesanías	stationery store	una papelería
post office	el correo	supermarket	un supermercado

Folk arts and crafts to buy

bark painting	el amate	key ring	el llavero
basket	la canasta	maracas	las maracas
blanket	el sarape	mask	la máscara
box	la caja	mug	el tarro
bracelet	la pulsera	overblouse	el huipil
chess set	el (tablero de) ajedrez	poncho	el jorongo/ poncho
cooking pot	la cazuela	pottery	la cerámica
dress	el vestido	ring	el anillo
earrings	los aretes	rug	el tapete
flower	la flor	sandals	los huaraches
flower pot	la maceta	shawl	el rebozo
glass	el vaso	shirt	la camisa
guitar	la guitarra	white cotton shirt-jacket	la guayabera
hammock	la hamaca		
handicrafts	las artesanías	sugar skull	la calavera de azúcar
hat	el sombrero		
jewelry	la joyería	textiles	los textiles
jug	la jarra	tray	la charola
earthenware jug	el jarro	wine glass	la copa

59

BUYING THINGS

Materials

What is it made of?	¿De qué está hecho/a?
What are they made of?	¿De qué están hechos/as?
Is it made of . . . ?	¿Está hecho/a de . . . ?
Are they made of . . . ?	¿Están hechos/as de . . . ?
a (silver/alpaca/gold) ring	un anillo de (plata/alpaca/oro)

brass	**latón**	papier mâché	**papier mâché**
copper	**cobre**	silver	**plata**
cotton	**algodón**	straw	**paja**
earthenware	**barro**	tin-plate	**hojalata**
(hand-blown)	**vidrio (soplado)**	turquoise	**turquesa**
glass		wicker	**mimbre**
gold	**oro**	wood	**madera**
leather	**cuero/piel**	wool	**lana**
cut-out paper	**papel picado**		

How are they made?

Es hecho/a* a mano.	It's handmade.
Son hechos/as* a mano.	They're handmade.

carved	**tallado/a**	lacquered	**laqueado/a**
embroidered	**bordado/a**	painted	**pintado/a**
knitted	**tejido/a**		

* If you want to be really accurate with masculine/feminine, singular/plural, check in Language builder, p108.

BUYING THINGS

Buying food

apple	**una manzana**	lemon	**un limón***
apricot	**un chabacano***	lettuce	**una lechuga**
artichoke	**una alcachofa**	lime	**un limón**
asparagus	**unos espárragos**	mango	**el mango**
avocado	**un aguacate***	melon	**un melón**
banana	**un plátano***	mushrooms	**los hongos, los champiñones**
basil	**la albahaca**		
beans	**unos frijoles***		
cabbage	**la col**	onion	**una cebolla**
carrot	**una zanahoria**	orange	**una naranja**
cauliflower	**una coliflor**	peach	**un durazno**
celery	**un apio**	peas	**los chícharos***
chick peas	**unos garbanzos**	parsley	**el perejil**
coriander	**el cilantro**	passion fruit	**el maracuyá***
corn	**el maíz***	pepper	**el pimiento***
cucumber	**un pepino**	pear	**una pera**
eggplant	**una berenjena**	pineapple	**una piña, un ananá**
fig	**un higo**		
garlic	**el ajo**	plantain	**un plátano macho**
grapefruit	**una toronja***		
grapes (black)	**unas uvas negras**	plum	**una ciruela**
		potato	**una papa**
grapes (green)	**unas uvas verdes**	radish	**un rábano**
		strawberries	**las fresas***
green beans	**unos ejotes**	tomato	**el tomate, el jitomate***
hot pepper	**el chile***		
leek	**el poro**	watermelon	**la sandía**

* Many food items have different names throughout Central and South America. You may find that locals use words other than those listed here.

BUYING THINGS

chiles

Unusual fruits and vegetables

la caña	sugar cane
la jícama	yam bean
los nopales	young cactus
la flor de calabaza	zucchini flower
la papaya	papaya
la guanábana	soursop
la tuna	prickly pear
la guayaba	guava
el zapote	sapodilla plum
el huitlacoche	corn smut

Buying groceries

bread	el pan	margarine	la margarina
butter	la mantequilla	milk	la leche
cake	el pastel	oil	el aceite
cheese	el queso	tea	el té negro
coffee	el café	yogurt	el yogurt
cookies	las galletas	(red/white/rosé) wine	el vino (tinto/blanco/rosado)
ham	el jamón		
(orange) juice	el jugo de (naranja)		

Weights, measures

1kg	un kilo	100g	cien gramos
0.5kg	medio kilo	1 liter	un litro
0.25kg	un cuarto (de kilo)	a dozen	una docena
		half a dozen	media docena

Containers

bag	una bolsa	can	una lata
bottle	una botella	jar	un frasco
box	una caja	packet	un paquete

BUYING THINGS

Trying on and buying clothes

I'd like (a sweater/boots).	**Quisiera (un suéter/unas botas).**
size . . .	**talla . . .** (for clothes)
	número . . . (for shoes)
Can I try it on?	**¿Puedo probármelo/la?***
Can I try them on?	**¿Puedo probármelos/las?**
It's a bit (big/small).	**Está algo (grande/chico/a).**
They're a bit (big/small).	**Están algo (grandes/chicos/as).**
Do you have any in green?	**¿Tiene (uno(s)/una(s))* en verde?**
(See p35 for colors.)	
How much (is it/are they)?	**¿Cuánto (cuesta/cuestan)?**
I like (it/them).	**Me (gusta/gustan).**
I'll take it.	**Me (lo/la) llevo.**
I'll take them.	**Me (los/las) llevo.**
Do you take credit cards?	**¿Se aceptan tarjetas de crédito?**

Claro.	Of course.
Pase por aquí.	Come this way.
Le (queda/quedan) bien.	(It/they) suit you.
No, solamente efectivo.	No, cash only.

* If you want to be really accurate with masculine/feminine, singular/plural, check in Language builder, p108.

zapatos

BUYING THINGS

Items of clothing

English	Spanish	English	Spanish
bathing suit	**el traje de baño††**	pants	**los pantalones**
belt	**el cinturón**	sandals	**las sandalias, los huaraches** (rougher, peasant type)
blouse	**la blusa**		
boots	**las botas**		
boxer shorts	**los boxers, los calzones**	shirt	**la camisa**
		shoes	**los zapatos**
bra	**el brasier***	shorts	**los shorts**
briefs	**los calzoncillos**	skirt	**la falda**
		stockings	**las medias**
coat	**el abrigo**	sweater	**el suéter**
dress	**el vestido**	T-shirt	**la playera/ la camiseta**
hat	**el sombrero**		
jacket	**el saco**	tie	**la corbata**
jacket, bomber	**la chamarra†**	tights	**las pantimedias**
jeans	**los jeans**	underpants	**las pantaletas****

* Central America/Argentina **el sostén/el corpiño**
† Argentina **la campera**
** Argentina/Cuba **las bombachas/el blumer**
†† Cuba **la trusa**

small	**chico/a/os/as**
medium	**mediano/a/os/as**
large	**grande/s**

Material

a leather jacket	**una chamarra de piel**
a (wool/cotton/silk) sweater	**un suéter de (lana/algodón/seda)**

At the newsstand

Do you have any (American/English) newspapers?	**¿Tiene periódicos (americanos/ingleses)?**
foreign newspapers	**los periódicos extranjeros**
magazines	**las revistas**
map	**el mapa**
postcards	**las tarjetas postales**

Buying and developing film

a roll of (color/black and white) film	**un rollo (a colores/en blanco y negro)**
for (prints/slides)	**para (fotos/diapositivas)**
a battery	**una pila**
Will you develop this film?	**¿Me revela este rollo?**
When will it be ready?	**¿Para cuándo está listo?**

BUYING THINGS

Language works

Shopping at the craft market

1 The price is right
- ¿Qué desea?
- ¿Cuánto cuesta este anillo?
- Cien pesos.
- Es muy caro.
- Es de plata. Mire, está quintado.
- Sí, pero es muy caro. Le doy ochenta.
- ¿Va a llevar algo más?
- Estos aretes.
- Bueno, noventa.

(**está quintado** = it's hallmarked)

How much did you bring the price down?

At the food market

2 You buy the fruit you want – almost
- Buenos días. ¿Tiene mangos?
- Perdone, no tenemos.
- ¿A cómo están las naranjas?
- A doce el kilo.
- Deme dos kilos, y una papaya.
- ¿Algo más?
- No, gracias. ¿Cuánto es?

Why didn't you get mangoes?
How much did you pay for the oranges?

Buying clothes

3 You get the right fit
- Quisiera esa playera.
- ¿Ésta?
- Sí, talla mediana.
- La tenemos en rojo y en azul.
- En azul. ¿Puedo probármela?
- Claro que sí. Pase por aquí.

What colors are available?

Buying an English language newspaper

4 You go to the *puesto de periódicos* thinking of home
- Buenas tardes, ¿tiene periódicos ingleses?
- No, pero tengo *The News*. Es mexicano pero está en inglés.
- ¿Y revistas?
- Tengo *Newsweek* y *Time*.
- Deme *The News* y *Time*.

What is *The News*?

Having film developed

5 You are dying to see your photos
- ¿Me revela este rollo?
- Sí, claro.
- ¿Para cuándo está listo?
- Para mañana en la tarde.
- Bueno.
- ¿A qué nombre?

When can you see your photos?

BUYING THINGS

Sound check

Spoken Spanish sounds very fast because words are usually linked together.

If a word ends in a vowel and the following word starts with the same vowel, the two vowels are pronounced as one, so the two words are joined together:
¿Dónde_está?

If a word ends in a vowel and the following word starts with another vowel, the two words are pronounced as one syllable, joining the words together:
Está_en la planta baja.

Practice saying these phrases:
Quisiera una falda.
¿En que piso está?
Una camisa de algodón.

Try it out

Food mixer

Rearrange the syllables in these words to make things you can eat or drink.

goju   tanoplá   mónja
díasan   chocaalfa   soque
vohue   janaran   chele
chulega

Phrase matcher

Match each of the phrases (1–5) with the best reply (a–e).
1 ¿Le gusta?
2 ¿Algo más?
3 ¿Qué talla?
4 ¿Cuánto quiere?
5 ¿Cuánto es?

a Grande.
b Deme medio kilo.
c Sí, pero prefiero el azul.
d Doscientos treinta pesos.
e No, nada más, gracias.

As if you were there

You are buying souvenirs at a handicrafts shop
☐ **¿Le gusta la charola?**
■ (Say it's very nice and ask what it's made of)
☐ **Es de madera laqueada . . . pintada a mano.**
■ (Ask the price)
☐ **Doscientos veinte pesos.**
■ (Ask if they take credit cards)
☐ **No, solamente efectivo.**
■ (Ask if it's her best price)
☐ **Sí, es precio fijo.**
■ (Decide whether to take it or whether it's too expensive)

Café life

You can be forgiven for spending much of your time in Mexico's excellent cafés and bars. A simple black coffee is known as either a *café americano* or a *café negro*; many cafés have espresso machines (*café espresso*).

The distinction between a *café con leche* and a *café con crema* is that the former is served with hot milk mixed in, while the latter arrives with a separate small jug of room-temperature cream (or, increasingly likely, a tiny plastic container).

! I'd like a coffee with cream.
Un café con leche.

Aficionados of tea (*té*) are advised that it is rarely prepared well in Mexico.

You can usually judge prices by the appearance of a place; white-gloved waiters imply high prices (with tips to match), while most places frequented by locals are cheap and cheerful.

Once you move into the realm of alcoholic drinks, you should proceed with caution. First, in your choice of venue: in the typically rough *cantina*, women may feel uncomfortable or positively vulnerable. Second, in your choice of company: many Mexicans, especially habitués of bars, are gregarious in the extreme and welcoming towards visitors. If you do not wish to become embroiled in a hard-drinking session, decline offers of drinks politely. Cocktail bars, particularly those in hotels, are usually salubrious.

Drinks to try

Beer The standard drink in Mexico is *cerveza*, sold always ice-cold and usually with a glass (as opposed to the trend in non-Latin countries to drink Mexican beer straight from the bottle with a segment of lime in the neck).

Tequila, much of it made in the town of the same name (see p15), is distilled from the hearts of *agave*, a kind of cactus. The "gold" version is the same as the clear or "silver" variety but with coloring added. In bars, it is generally served with a lime segment and salt. The theory is that you sprinkle salt on the back of your wrist, suck the lime, swallow the Tequila, lick the salt and repeat *ad nauseam*.

Mezcal is similar in origin to Tequila, though made with a wider range of cacti and often with a worm added to each bottle.

Wine made locally has improved rapidly, and the finest now match those of California. Be warned that red wine is often served inappropriately chilled.

Mineral water is widely available, and mostly palatable.

Fruit juices are usually excellent, with a variety of tropical fruits combined with each other, sugar or milk.

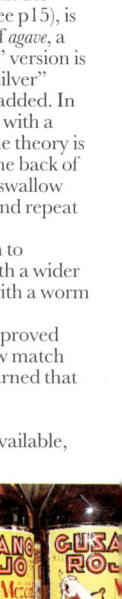

CAFÉ LIFE

Phrasemaker

Places to have a drink or snack

un bar – bar
un café – cafe
una cantina – bar (in some of the more working-class ones, women might not be welcome)
jugos, licuados – juice or liquidized fruit drink, or the sign outside establishments selling them
una nevería – establishment which sells ice cream, sorbets and often fruit juices
una lonchería – simple establishment selling regional fast food and soft drinks
un puesto – a stall
una taquería – sells tacos (see p71) of various kinds

Asking what there is

Do you have any (ice cream/tacos)?	**¿Tienen (helado/tacos)?**
What (ice cream/tacos) do you have?	**¿De qué tiene (el helado/los tacos)?**
What (cold/hot) drinks do you have?	**¿Qué bebidas (frías/calientes) tiene?**
What (bottled) soft drinks do you have?	**¿Qué refrescos (embotellados) tiene?**

Clarifying

What is "mezcal"?	**¿Qué es el mezcal?**
What are "quesadillas"?	**¿Qué son las quesadillas?**
What is "pulque" like?	**¿Cómo es el pulque?**
Is it (very) spicy?	**¿Pica (mucho)?**
Has the salad been disinfected?	**¿La ensalada está desinfectada?**
Is it purified water?	**¿Es agua purificada?**
It's a typical dish. It's made with (chicken).	**Es un plato típico, lleva (pollo).**
(It's/They're) a sort of . . .	**(Es/Son) una especie de . . .**
Yes, it's (a bit) hot.	**Sí, pica (un poco).**
No, it's not hot.	**No, no pica.**

CAFÉ LIFE

Ordering

I'd like . . .	**Quisiera . . .**
I'd like a ham (roll/sandwich).	**Me da (una torta/un sandwich) de jamón.**
I'd like two (beefsteak/chicken) tacos.	**Me da dos tacos de (bistec/pollo).**
with everything	**con todo**
without (onion/hot peppers)	**sin (cebolla/chile)**
to carry out	**para llevar**
to eat in	**para comer aquí**

Sí, cómo no.	Yes, of course.
¿Qué va a tomar?	What are you going to have?
¿Con todo?	With all the trimmings?
¿Es todo?	Is that everything?
¿(Qué quiere/Quiere algo) de beber?	(What would you like/Would you like something) to drink?
Perdone, no tenemos.	Sorry, we don't have any.

Paying

How much is it?	**¿Cuánto es?**
Here you are.	**Aquí tiene.**
My change?	**¿Mi cambio?**

Snacks

cheese	**el queso**
chicken	**el pollo**
hamburger	**una hamburguesa**
hot dog	**un perro caliente/un hot dog**
leg of pork	**una pierna de puerco**
olives	**unas aceitunas**
pâté	**el paté**
peanuts	**unos cacahuates**
pizza	**una pizza**
popcorn	**unas palomitas**
pork chop	**una chuleta**
potato chips	**unas papas fritas**
pumpkin seeds	**unas pepitas**
sandwich	**un sandwich**
rib	**una costilla**
veal escalope	**una milanesa**

Specialty snacks

un buñuelo – a flat, round version of **churros**, served with raw cane syrup
un churro – elongated, deep-fried fritter covered with sugar
un elote (con mantequilla/queso/mayonesa) – corn on the cob (with butter/cheese/mayonnaise)
(pepino/mango/naranja/jícama) con (limón/sal/chile) – (cucumber/mango/orange/yam bean) with (lime/salt/hot peppers)
una quesadilla – folded tortilla filled with cheese (although nowadays there is a variety of fillings)
un sope – a thick tortilla, sold with salsa, cheese and onion on top
un taco – rolled up tortilla with a variety of fillings
un tamal – cornmeal- or banana-leaf-wrapped parcel of cornmeal, filled with meat if savory or raisins if sweet
una torta – a large roll with a main filling complemented with tomato, avocado, hot peppers, butter beans and cream
una tortilla – cornmeal pancake

Cold drinks

un agua mineral (con gas/sin gas)	a (carbonated/noncarbonated) mineral water
un jugo de (naranja/piña)	(orange/pineapple) juice
una (limonada/naranjada)	(lemonade/orangeade)
un refresco	a (usually bottled) soft drink
un agua de (jamaica/tamarindo)	water flavored with (hibiscus/tamarind)
un vaso de leche	a glass of milk
un licuado de (papaya/melón)	drink made with water and liquidized fruit (papaya/melon)
una malteada	drink made with milk and liquidized fruit or ice cream
un té helado	iced tea

Hot drinks

café negro	black coffee
café con leche	coffee with cream
café descafeinado	decaffeinated coffee
café de olla	black coffee with raw cane sugar and cinnamon
capuchino	cappuccino
té negro con limón o con crema	tea with lemon or cream (specify **con leche** if you want it with milk)
té de manzanilla	camomile infusion
chocolate	chocolate

Ice cream and sorbets

el helado	ice cream
la nieve	sorbet
un barquillo de . . .	a . . . cone
un vaso de . . .	a . . . cup
una paleta de . . .	a . . . popsicle

ananá	pineapple	**mango**	mango
banana	banana	**melón**	melon
chocolate	chocolate	**naranja**	orange
coco	coconut	**piña**	pineapple
elote	sweet corn	**pistache**	pistachio
fresa	strawberry	**plátano (y nuez)**	banana (and walnut)
guanábana	soursop		
limón	lemon (lime in Mexico)	**rompope**	eggnog
		vainilla	vanilla

Alcoholic drinks

(a bottle/half a bottle/a glass) of	**(una botella/media botella/una copa) de**
(dry/sweet) (red/white/rosé) wine	**vino (tinto/blanco/rosado) (seco/dulce)**
(dark/light) beer	**una cerveza (oscura/clara)**
cognac	**un coñac**
gin	**una ginebra**
gin and tonic	**un gin and tonic**
Kahlúa (Mexican coffee liqueur)	**un Kahlúa**
margarita	**un margarita**
(dry) martini	**un martini (seco)**
(carbonated/noncarbonated) mineral water	**agua mineral (con gas/ sin gas)**
rum	**un ron**
rum and coke	**una cuba**
tequila (with a tomato and orange chaser)	**un tequila (y una sangrita)**
piña colada	**una piña colada**
vermouth	**un vermut**
vodka	**un vodka**
whisky	**un whisky**
neat	**solo**
on the rocks	**en las rocas**
with (water/soda)	**con (agua/soda)**
with a twist of lemon	**con una rebanadita de limón**

Specialty drinks

coco loco – a green coconut with the top cut off, then one or more spirits, a dash of lemon and ice are added to the coconut milk
chicha – strong drink made from fermented fruit juices or corn
guarapo – sugar-cane juice
mezcal – distilled cactus juice (some kinds are bottled with a worm at the bottom)
pulque – fermented cactus juice
sangría – a mixture of red wine, lemonade and fruit pieces

CAFÉ LIFE

Sound check

Spanish has some letters that don't exist in other languages:

ñ
Pronounced like the **ni** in "onion."
champaña *champania*
coñac *koniak*

Practice on these words
España   mañana   señorita

ll
Pronounced like **y** in "yes."
calle *kaye*
allí *ayee*

Practice on these words
lleno   calle   quesadilla

Language works

A nice day for a picnic

1 You are having a picnic, so you go and get *tortas*
- ¿De qué tiene tortas?
- De pollo, de jamón y de bistec.
- Me da dos de jamón y dos de pollo, por favor.
- ¿Con todo?
- Sin chile.

What can the rolls be filled with?

Sampling *tacos al carbón*

2 You and a friend are standing at the grill
- Dos tacos, por favor.
- ¿De bistec o de chuleta?
- De bistec. Y dos refrescos.
- Sí, jefe/a. ¿Qué refresco quieren?
- ¿Qué tienen?
(**jefe/jefa** = boss (not ironical))

What does the taco maker ask you?

Ordering drinks

3 You have to change your order slightly
- ¿Qué quiere de beber?
- Un agua mineral con gas y una Corona Extra.
- Perdone, no tenemos Corona. En cerveza clara tenemos Dos Equis y Bohemia.
- Bohemia, por favor.

Why did you ask for a "Bohemia"?

A drink on the beach

4 The sun is hot, the sea is blue and a drink would be just the thing
- ¿Quiere algo de beber?
- Sí, ¿tiene cocos?
- Sí, ¿le traigo un coco preparado?
- ¿Un coco loco?
- Sí, con ginebra.
- Bien. Un coco loco y una cuba.

What do they put in their coco loco?

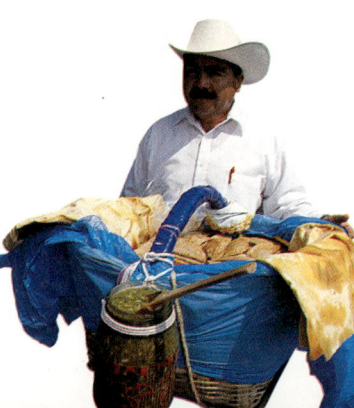

Try it out

Crossword

Write the Spanish names of the five ice-cream flavors across the grid to help you find the drink America introduced to Europe.

1 Pistachio   4 Strawberry
2 Mango   5 Corn
3 Melon

Split the difference

Combine these halves of words and then find two that are not drinks.

te   cafeinado   re   monada
ca   go   li   fresco   chu
gría   san   quila   des   veza
cafeinado   mar   rro   ju
garita   cer   cahuate

As if you were there

You and your friend have been sightseeing all afternoon, so you need a rest and some sustenance. You go into a café.

☐ **Buenas tardes, ¿Qué van a tomar?**
■ (Ask for a tea with milk for your friend and what soft drinks they have)
☐ **Tenemos Coca, Sprite, malteada.**
■ (Ask for the drink you want)
☐ **¿Es todo?**
■ (Ask for two *buñuelos*)
☐ **Perdone, no tenemos.**
■ (Ask for some *churros*)

Eating out

Perhaps the greatest pleasure of a visit to Mexico is the quality and variety of the nation's food. From a simple snack at a roadside shack, to an evening of fine dining in a chic restaurant, it is easy to find good-value food and drink. It is common practice to leave a tip of 10% for the waiter/waitress in Mexico. Many people leave a few coins or round up the bill; however, US-style tips of around 15% are becoming the norm in resorts like Cancún and Puerto Vallarta.

❗ Is there a good restaurant near here?
🔴 ¿Hay un buen restaurante por aquí?

Meals

Breakfast (*desayuno*) is normally a simple affair of fruit juice, coffee, bread or toast with jam, and perhaps an egg dish; in fancier hotels, though, it may comprise an expansive buffet with everything from fresh fruit to chicken stew! *Desayuno americano* is usually an egg-based dish. The main meal of the day is lunch (*comida*), begun at around 2 pm (though some office workers start earlier). Dinner (*cena*) starts at around 8 pm or 9 pm, though in a reasonably sized town you can also find somewhere to serve you at midnight or beyond.

Where to eat

The best value is usually found at modest establishments, which may be individual restaurants or comprise part of a bigger enterprise – cafeterias in department stores are often surprisingly good. They also cater well to children; in these and most other restaurants, considerable

efforts will be made to ensure the comfort of young children and to prepare special dishes for them.

Types of food

Most meals are straightforward three-course affairs, with an appetizer, main course (usually served with rice) and a dessert. Meat is a staple, as is fish in coastal areas, but the needs of vegetarians are being addressed in larger cities and resorts. Fast-food outlets are hugely popular among young Mexicans.

A basic element of Mexican food is the *tortilla*, made with either wheat or corn flour (a *taco* when filled). The filling comprises any or all of meat, seafood, beans or cheese. Beans (*frijoles*) are a specialty and a good source of protein and carbohydrates. They are most frequently served refried – boiled, mashed, fried and fried again.

If you have low spice tolerance, be sure to ask whether a dish contains a lot of hot peppers before you order anything in a non-tourist restaurant in Mexico – many dishes contain large (to a Western palate) quantities. Watch out also for salads – it is best to steer clear of them unless you are sure they have been disinfected.

> Is it very spicy?
> **¿Pica mucho?**

For such a large country, there is surprisingly little regional variation in cuisine. In general, though, the further south you go the greater the pre-Columbian influence.

Dishes to try

Ceviche, a tangy appetizer of seafood marinated in lime juice.
Sopa de aguacate, combining

avocado and cream in a delicious soup.
Gazpacho, a soup served cold like its Spanish counterpart but made spicier with the generous addition of hot peppers.
Guacamole, a mash of avocados, tomatoes and garlic, usually served on combination plates.
Huevos a la mexicana, where eggs are scrambled with green hot peppers, tomatoes and garlic to match the green, red and white of the Mexican flag.
Barbacoa, a dish with its origins in Mayan cuisine. A leg of meat (then venison, now lamb) is swaddled in cactus leaves and cooked slowly overnight.
Machaca, shredded beef or pork served with egg and spices to form a kind of meat hash.
Enchiladas, tortillas filled with chicken and sometimes served with *mole*, a sauce made from peanuts, spices, hot peppers and even chocolate.
Chongos zamoranos, a dessert of cottage cheese in syrup made from milk, cinnamon and sugar.
Ensalada de frutas, a simple but delicious fresh fruit salad.

EATING OUT

Phrasemaker

Finding a place to eat

Is there a good (restaurant/bar) near here?
¿Hay un buen (restaurante/bar) por aquí?
Is there a good cafeteria near here?
¿Hay una buena cafetería por aquí?

una fonda – restaurant that provides everyday typical Mexican food at reasonable prices
una hacienda – an old *hacienda* or large ranch that has been turned into a luxury hotel and/or restaurant
un restaurante – restaurant

Reserving a table

I'd like to reserve a table for two for (tonight/Tuesday).
Quisiera reservar una mesa para dos personas para (hoy en la noche/el martes).

at (eight/ eight thirty) **a (las ocho/las ocho y media)**
in the name of . . . **a nombre de . . .**

(See p32 and p35 for dates and times.)

Está bien.	That's fine.
(Perdone) no tenemos . . .	(Sorry) we don't have any . . .
No hace falta reservar.	There's no need to book.

Arriving

a table for (two/four) **una mesa para (dos/cuatro)**
by the window **junto a la ventana**
outside/inside **afuera/adentro**
in the (no) smoking area **en la sección de (no) fumar**
We have a reservation in the name of . . . **Tenemos una reservación, una reserva (Arg) a nombre de . . .**

Bienvenido(s).	Welcome.
(Pase) por aquí.	(Please come) this way.

Talking about the menu

waiter/waitress	**mesero/mesera***
The menu, please.	**La carta, por favor.**
Is there a set lunch menu?	**¿Hay menu del día?**
	¿Hay comida corrida? (in popular Mexican restaurants)
What's the set menu?	**¿Cuál es el menú del día?**
Do you have any (seafood/chicken)?	**¿Tienen (mariscos/pollo)?**
What is ("mole"/"molletes")?	**¿Qué es (mole/molletes)?**
What is "guacamole" like?	**¿Cómo es el guacamole?**
What are "huevos rancheros" like?	**¿Cómo son los huevos rancheros?**
What (does it/do they) contain?	**¿Qué llevan?**
Is it (very) spicy?	**¿Pica (mucho)?**
What's the soup of the day?	**¿Cuál es la sopa del día?**
What's the local specialty?	**¿Cuál es el plato típico de aquí?**
* Argentina	**mozo/moza**
Tenemos . . .	We have . . .
comida corrida	a set three/four course lunch, usually with a choice at each stage, for a reasonable price
menú turístico	as above, with tourists in mind
a la carta	à la carte
Perdone, no tenemos . . .	Sorry, we don't have any . . .
Es un plato típico, lleva pollo . . .	It's a typical dish. It's made with chicken . . .
Es una especie de . . .	It's a sort of . . .
Sí, pica (un poco).	Yes, it's (a bit) spicy.
No, no pica.	No, it's not spicy.
Se lo recomiendo.	I recommend it.

(See p73 for drinks.)

EATING OUT

Ordering

(A fish soup/chicken tacos) for me.	**Para mí (una sopa de pescado/ unos tacos de pollo).**
¿Les tomo su orden?	May I take your order?
¿Qué van a tomar?	What would you like?
para empezar	to start with
como plato principal	as a main course
de postre	for dessert
¿Cómo lo quiere?	How would you like it?
¿Van a tomar (postre/café)?	Would you like any (dessert/coffee)?
¿Quieren algo de beber?	Would you like anything to drink?
¿Y de beber?	Anything to drink?

Eating habits

I'm a vegetarian.	**Soy vegetariano/a.**
I don't eat (meat/hot peppers/seafood).	**No como (carne/chile/mariscos).**
Does it contain (salt/sugar/nuts)?	**¿Lleva (sal/azúcar/nueces)?**
I'm allergic to (fish/nuts).	**Soy alérgico/a (al pescado/a las nueces).**
Do you have any artificial sweetener?	**¿Tiene sacarina?**

At the table

cup	**una taza**	dish	**un plato**
fork	**un tenedor**	glass	**un vaso**
knife	**un cuchillo**	napkin	**una servilleta**
saucer	**un platito**	spoon	**una cuchara**
teaspoon	**una cucharita**	wine glass	**una copa**

During the meal

Where are the restrooms?	**¿Dónde están los baños?**
Has the salad been disinfected?	**¿La ensalada está desinfectada?**
Can I have (a knife/more bread), please?	**¿Me trae (un cuchillo/más pan) por favor?**
Is it purified water?	**¿Es agua purificada?**
It's (cold/raw).	**Está (frío/crudo).**
(It's/They're) very spicy!	**¡(Pica/Pican) mucho!**
This is not what I asked for.	**Esto no es lo que pedí.**
I asked for . . .	**Pedí . . .**
Can you change this (fork/dish)?	**¿Puede cambiarme este (tenedor/plato)?**
Damas/Mujeres	Ladies
Caballeros/Hombres	Men

Paying the bill

The check, please.	**La cuenta, por favor.**
Is the tip included?	**¿Está incluido el servicio?**
Do you take credit cards?	**¿Acepta tarjetas de crédito?**
There's a mistake.	**Hay un error.**
We didn't have this.	**No tomamos esto.**
Keep the change.	**Quédese con el cambio.**

EATING OUT

Sound check

g + **e** or **i** is pronounced like **ch** in "Loch Ness."
Argentina *arhhehnteenah*
ginebra *hheenehbrah*

g + **ue** or **ui** is pronounced like **g** in "gun." In these cases, the **u** is silent.
guitarra *gitahrrah*
portugués *poartoogehs*

g + any other combination of letters is pronounced like **g** in "gun," with all the following letters pronounced.
agua *ahgooah*
gracias *grahseeahs*

Practice with these words:
**guacamole Gibraltar hígado
guitarra gelatina guía
algo langosta**

guacamole

Language works

Better safe than sorry

1 You call to reserve a table
☐ **Hacienda de Los Morales, buenas tardes.**
■ **Buenas tardes, quisiera reservar una mesa para mañana en la noche.**
☐ **Mañana en la noche . . . , perdone pero no tenemos en la noche.**
■ **¿Para el jueves?**
☐ **Para el jueves . . . está bien, señor(ita). ¿Para cuántas personas?**
■ **Para tres, a nombre de . . .**
☐ **Muy bien, una mesa para tres, para el jueves. ¿A qué hora?**
■ **Para las ocho.**
☐ **Bueno. Hasta el jueves, señor(ita).**

There aren't any tables available tomorrow night: true/false?

In a restaurant

2 Will you like what you order?
☐ **¿Y de plato principal?**
■ **¿Cómo es el huachinango a la veracruzana?**
☐ **Es un pescado al horno guisado con jitomate, cebolla, chiles y aceitunas. Se lo recomiendo.**

What is in *huachinango a la veracruzana*?

EATING OUT

At a cafeteria

3 You and a friend have been considering the menu
- ☐ ¿Les tomo su orden?
- ■ Sí. Ceviche y machaca. Y para mí . . . ¿La ensalada está desinfectada?
- ☐ Sí, claro.
- ■ Una ensalada César y . . . enchiladas suizas. ¿Pican mucho?
- ☐ No, no pican.
- ■ Bueno, unas enchiladas suizas.

Has the salad been disinfected?
Are the enchiladas hot?

Fruit for breakfast

4 You would like some fruit with your breakfast
- ☐ ¿Va a tomar café?
- ■ Sí, gracias.
- ☐ ¿Le tomo su orden?
- ■ ¿De qué tiene frutas?
- ☐ Piña, sandía y melón. Hay con yogurt y sin yogurt.
- ■ Con yogurt, por favor. Y unos huevos revueltos con jamón.

What fruit are you getting with your yogurt?

tortilla

Try it out

As if you were there

It's a lovely sunny morning. You have been for a walk by the sea and now you would like breakfast. Use the Menu reader on p84.

- ■ (Greet the waiter and say you'd like a table for two outside)
- ☐ **Muy bien. Por aquí.**

- ☐ **¿Qué van a tomar?**
- ■ (Ask for two orange juices, ham and eggs and waffles with maple syrup)
- ☐ **¿Quieren café, té?**
- ■ (Ask for two pots of coffee and a fork – there isn't one in your place setting)
- ☐ **Sí, cómo no.**
(**Cómo no** = But of course)

Menu reader

Specialties

gazpacho

arroz con pollo (Caribbean) rice with chicken and tomato
molletes con frijoles toasted halves of bread rolls spread with fried beans and topped with melted cheese
enchiladas (suizas/rojas) rolled tortillas filled with chicken or cheese and covered with (green tomato sauce/red tomato sauce) and cheese
guacamole avocado, puréed with chopped tomato, onion and hot peppers
hayacas (Venezuela) parcels of cornmeal dough filled with meat and vegetables, wrapped in banana leaves and steamed
pabellón criollo (Venezuela) rice, beans and meat stew
quesadillas (de queso/hongos, flor de calabaza/huitlacoche, etc.) folded tortillas with a (cheese/mushroom/zucchini flowers/corn smut, etc.) filling
mole (poblano/verde) meat, usually chicken, in a sauce made with herbs, nuts, spices and hot peppers (**poblano**: dark brown, with bitter chocolate in it; **verde**: with pumpkin seeds and green tomatoes)
moros y cristianos (literally Moors and Christians) a Caribbean dish combining dark beans with white rice
salsa (verde, roja, pico de gallo) sauce made with green or red tomatoes and hot peppers, can be cooked or raw – there will often be a bowl on typical restaurant tables, or you can ask for some. Be careful, salsa can be very hot.
tacos (de pollo/barbacoa) rolled tortillas with a (chicken/ lamb cooked slowly underground in cactus leaves) filling
   al carbón tacos filled with beef or pork char-grilled in front of you. A delicious, cheap and fast meal.
tamales parcels of cornmeal dough filled with meat and a sauce, wrapped in corn husks or banana leaves and steamed
   de dulce as above, but sweet, with raisins or other fruit instead of meat
tortillas cornmeal pancakes eaten in Mexico instead of bread
   de harina tortillas made with wheat flour
tostadas crispy tortillas topped with beans, lettuce, chicken or other meat, cheese, sour cream and salsa

MENU READER

Ways of cooking

a la plancha/a la parrilla grilled
a la moda with ice cream
al carbón char-grilled
al horno in the oven: baked, roasted
al mojo de ajo grilled, with garlic
asado roast
cocido boiled
crudo raw

empanizado breaded
en salsa in a sauce
guisado stewed
relleno stuffed
sin (ajo/chile) without (garlic/hot peppers)
bien cocido well done
término medio medium
poco cocido rare

Menu sections

Desayuno Breakfast
Entradas Appetizers, Starters
Sopas, consomés, caldos Soups, consommés, broths
Ensaladas Salads
Especialidades del mar Fish and seafood specialties
Especialidades de la parrilla Specialties from the grill

Pescado Fish
Carnes Meat
Caza y aves Game and poultry
Verduras y legumbres Vegetables and legumes
Postres Desserts
Fruta y nueces Fruit and nuts

MENU READER

The menu

brocheta de camarones shrimp brochette
brocheta de res beef brochette
cabrito kid
cacahuates peanuts
calabacitas zucchini
calamares squid
   en su tinta squid in their own ink
(caldo/consomé) de pollo chicken consommé
caldo tlalpeño chicken consommé with chicken strips and avocado
camarones prawns, shrimps
camote sweet potato
carne a la tampiqueña steak served with guacamole, a **quesadilla** and fried beans
carne de res beef
carnero lamb
carnitas pork cooked in large copper pots in its own fat
cebolla onion
cereales varios con leche different cereals with milk
ceviche fish "cooked" in lemon or lime juice, served with tomato, avocado, onion (and hot peppers in Mexico)
chabacano apricot
champiñones mushrooms
chancho pork
chícharos peas
chile (poblano, jalapeño, chipotle, serrano) (poblano,

aguacate avocado
   relleno de (camarón/jaiba) avocado, stuffed with (shrimps/crab)
ají red pepper
ajo garlic
alcachofas artichokes
almejas clams
almendras almonds
ananá pineapple
anticucho char-grilled skewers of beef heart, served with a hot sauce
arroz (a la mexicana/blanco) rice (Mexican style with tomato/ without tomato)
ate de (membrillo/guayaba) (quince/guava) purée jelly
atún tuna
avena porridge
bacalao cod (usually dried)
banana banana
barbacoa leg of lamb wrapped in cactus leaves and cooked slowly overnight
batata sweet potato
berenjena eggplant
betabel beetroot
bife (a caballo) steak (topped with two fried eggs)
bisquets con mantequilla y miel toasted scones with butter and honey
bistec beefsteak
boquerones whitebait

MENU READER

ensalada

jalapeno, chipotle, serrano) hot peppers
chinchulines chitterlings
chipi chipi soup made with tiny clams
chirimoya custard apple
chongos zamoranos dessert made from milk, cinnamon and sugar
chorizo highly spiced pork sausage
chuleta chop
chupe de (camarones/mariscos) soup made with milk, peppers, eggs, and shrimps or seafood
churrasco large grilled steak
ciruela plum
ciruela pasa prune
cocktail/coctel de (camarones/ostiones) (shrimp/oyster) cocktail
coco coconut
col cabbage
coliflor cauliflower
conejo rabbit
costilla rib
crema de tomate tomato soup
crepas de cajeta pancakes with burnt milk candy
damasco apricot
ejotes green beans
elote corn
enchilada tortilla filled with chicken and served with a sauce made from vegetables or peppers
ensalada salad
  César Caesar salad
  de atún/pollo (tuna/chicken) salad
  de espinaca y tocino spinach and bacon salad
  de frutas fresh fruit salad
  mixta mixed salad
  verde green salad
espaguetis a la mantequilla spaghetti in butter sauce
espinacas spinach
faisán pheasant
fajitas de filete miñón strips of filet mignon sautéed with onions and peppers, served with flour tortillas
filete fillet steak
  de pescado al mojo de ajo fillet of fish sautéed with garlic
flan de coco y napolitano coconut or Neapolitan crème caramel
flor de calabaza zucchini flowers
frambuesa raspberry
fresa strawberry
frijoles beans
fruta de la estación fruit in season
garbanzos chick peas
gazpacho cold, spicy soup made with tomatoes
gelatina flavored gelatin
granada pomegranate
guacamole mash of avocados, tomatoes, onions and coriander
guajolote turkey
guanábana soursop
guayaba guava
habas broad beans
hamburguesa hamburger
helado de (vainilla/fresa/chocolate) (vanilla/strawberry/chocolate) ice cream

huevos rancheros

87

torta de huevos

(higaditos, pechuga, pierna) de pollo chicken (livers, breast, drumstick)
hígado liver
higo fig
hot cakes con cajeta o miel de maple pancakes with milk candy or maple syrup
huachinango red snapper
  a la veracruzana red snapper in a tomato sauce
  al horno baked red snapper
huevos eggs
  (fritos/revueltos) (fried/scrambled) eggs
  a la mexicana/mexicanos eggs scrambled with a tomato and pepper sauce
  rancheros fried eggs, served on tortillas and covered in tomato and pepper sauce
huitlacoche corn smut (a black fungus which grows on corn)
jaiba rellena stuffed crab
jaibas crab
jamón ham
jícama yam bean
jitomate tomato
langosta lobster
  termidor lobster thermidor
langostinos crayfish
lechuga lettuce
lenguado sole
limón lemon
limón lime (used in the place of lemon in Mexico)
lomo loin
machaca shredded beef or pork served with egg and spices
mandarina tangerine
mango mango
marrano pork
melón melon
mermelada jam (a variety of fruits)
  de naranja marmalade
mero bass
mojarra type of sea bream, tilapia fish
naranja orange
nieve de (limón/piña) (lemon/pineapple) sorbet
nopales, nopalitos young, fleshy leaf of the prickly pear cactus
nuez (de Castilla) walnut
ostiones oysters
pan bread
  dulce a selection of cakes, pastries and croissants
  francés slices of bread dipped in egg and fried in butter
  tostado con mantequilla y mermelada toast with butter and jam
papas potatoes
parrillada Machu Picchu steak served with avocado, pineapple and papaya
pato duck
pavo turkey
(pay/pie) de (queso/piña/manzana) (cheese/pineapple/apple) pie
(pay/pie) a la moda pie with ice cream
pepino cucumber
petits pois peas
pez espada swordfish
pierna leg
pimientos peppers
piña pineapple
plátano banana
macho plantain

plato de fruta con yogurt
plate of fruit with yogurt
plato de fruta de la estació
plate of fruit in season
pollo chicken
pomelo grapefruit
pozole a chicken or pork broth with cornmeal to which you can add oregano, lettuce, chopped radish
pulpo octopus
puerco pork
queso fundido grilled cheese
rábanos radishes
riñones kidneys
robalo sea bass
salchichas sausages
salmonete red mullet
sandía watermelon
sardinas sardines
sopa soup
  de aguacate avocado and cream soup
  de fideo vermicelli (pasta) in a tomato broth
  de lentejas lentil soup
  de tortilla chicken or tomato broth with tortilla strips or dumplings, served with avocado and sour cream and/or cheese
  de verduras vegetable soup
  del día soup of the day
tamarindo tamarind
ternera veal
tomate green tomato
toronja grapefruit
trucha trout
tuna prickly pear
venado venison
viudo de pescado
fish stew, cooked in a hole in the ground
waffles con miel de maple
waffles with maple syrup
zanahoria carrot

ensalada y tortillas

Drinks

aguas frescas (de jamaica/ tamarindo etc) flavored water (with hibiscus, etc)
cafe coffee
  americano cup of not-very-strong coffee, milk/cream will be brought separately
  de olla black coffee with raw cane sugar and cinnamon
  descafeinado decaffeinated coffee
capuchino cappucino
chicha strong drink made from fermented fruit juices or cornmeal
chocolate hot chocolate
jugo de naranja orange juice
jugo de toronja grapefruit juice
leche milk
mezcal distilled cactus juice; some kinds are bottled with a worm at the bottom
té tea
  con crema tea with cream
  con leche tea with milk
  negro con limón
tea with lemon
pulque fermented cactus juice
sangría a mixture of red wine, lemonade and fruit pieces

Salsa!

Entertainment and leisure

Cultural events

The main social activity in any Mexican town is the evening promenade around the main square, and participating in this is something that many visitors relish at the end of each day: language is no barrier when you join the swirl of humanity.

For a more structured form of entertainment, the most accessible is the movie theater – you can find one in even the smallest of towns. Most English-language films are subtitled in Spanish (compared with television programs, which are usually dubbed, often clumsily), but you may find that gory violence is the standard fare in many movies.

> Are there any movie theaters?
> ¿Hay cines?

The biggest cities are the most likely places to find good theater, too. Mexico has many fine auditoria, but these days there is a paucity of interesting drama. A good alternative is dance: the Ballet Folklórico, based in Mexico City, demonstrates how traditional Indian dance has been fused with modern techniques.

In terms of music, you will not travel far before mariachi bands begin to encroach. This is normally a happy experience, with singers, guitarists and brass players circulating around city squares and popular restaurants. In the clubs, there is a constant clash between American/British dance music and Latin influences, especially *salsa* from New York-based *latinos* and *cumbia* from Colombia.

ENTERTAINMENT AND LEISURE

Activities

Many visitors to Mexico are content to make the most of the country's excellent Caribbean and Pacific beaches; besides swimming in blissfully warm waters, opportunities for divers and sailors are excellent too. All-inclusive resorts, particularly around Cancún and Puerto Vallarta, offer a wide range of water- and land-based activities, from windsurfing to tennis.

> Can I rent a windsurf board?
> ¿Se puede alquilar una tabla de wind-surf?

Neither hiking nor cycling can yet be said to be a mainstream activity, though the prospects for both are excellent in rural areas. Experienced equestrians could also ask local people about the possibility of renting out a horse; much of the terrain is ideal for riding, and horses are still used professionally in much of the country.

The topology in Mexico does not easily lend itself to golf, but there are numerous courses on the Yucatán Peninsula. Green fees are significantly lower than in the US.

Spectator sports

That Mexico is the only country to have hosted soccer's World Cup twice since the Second World War says much about the nation's obsession with *futbol*. Mexico's national team is in the top flight of soccer-playing nations, and its domestic competitions are fiercely fought. The best teams are in Mexico City and Guadalajara, but almost every street in every town has an impromptu field.

Most foreign visitors find a game of soccer more palatable than the other great national sport, bullfighting.

For children

In a globe-trotting child's assessment of entertainment innovation, Mexico would not rate especially highly. The country lacks amenities with the scale and imagination of the Disney theme parks, and the best you can hope for is some fairly average water parks in resort areas. Some cities, though, possess a range of activities for the older child, with good hands-on museums and well-organized zoos.

ENTERTAINMENT AND LEISURE

Phrasemaker

Getting to know the place

Do you have (a map of the town/an entertainment guide)?	¿Tiene (un plano de la ciudad/una guía de espectáculos)?
Do you have (information/a guidebook) in English?	¿Tiene (información/una guía) en inglés?
Are there any (movie theaters/concerts)?	¿Hay (cines/conciertos)?
Are films dubbed or do they have subtitles?	¿Las películas son dobladas o tienen subtítulos?
What is there (to see/to do) here?	¿Qué hay para (ver/hacer) aquí?
Is there (a guided tour/a bus tour)?	¿Hay (una visita con guía/un tour)?
Is there anything for children?	¿Hay algo para niños?
I like (waterskiing/music).	Me gusta (esquiar/la música).
I (like/don't like) bullfights.	(Me gustan/No me gustan) las corridas de toros.
I'm interested in (archaeology/folklore).	Me interesa (la arqueología/el folklor).
Can you recommend a nightclub?	¿Puede recomendarme un nightclub*?
I'd like to go to (a concert/the movies).	Me gustaría ir (a un concierto/al cine).
* Argentina	una boite

Hay una visita con guía (todos los días/los fines de semana).	There's a guided tour (every day/at weekends).
Hay ruinas muy interesantes.	There are some very interesting ruins.
¿Le gusta (la salsa/la música mexicana)?	Do you like (salsa/Mexican music)?
Le recomiendo . . .	I'd recommend . . .

(For days of the week, see p35.)

ENTERTAINMENT AND LEISURE

Things to do and places to see

art gallery	**una galería de arte**
(folklore) ballet	**el ballet (folklórico)**
beach	**la playa**
open bar	**una barra libre**
boat trip	**un paseo en barco**
bullfight	**una corrida de toros**
castle	**el castillo**
cathedral	**la catedral**

church	**el templo/la iglesia**
cobbled streets	**las calles empedradas**
concert	**un concierto**
dance hall	**un salón de baile**
discotheque	**una discoteca**
(art/painting/ceramics) exhibition	**una exhibición (de arte/de pintura/de cerámica)**
fair	**una feria**
fiesta	**una fiesta**
fireworks	**los fuegos artificiales**
market	**el mercado**
miniature golf	**un golfito**
monument	**un monumento**
movie theater	**el cine**
museum	**el museo**
(music) festival	**un festival (de música)**
opera	**la ópera**
palace	**el palacio**
park	**el parque**
pyramids	**las pirámides**
river	**el río**
ruins	**las ruinas**
show	**un espectáculo**
soccer match	**un partido de futbol**
swimming pool	**una alberca**
theater	**un teatro**
ticket office	**la taquilla***
Tourist Office	**la Oficina de Turismo**
(video) games	**(vídeo) juegos**
waterfall	**la cascada**
* Argentina	**la ventanilla**

93

ENTERTAINMENT AND LEISURE

Getting more information

Where is (the swimming pool/the museum)?	¿Dónde está (la alberca/el museo)?
Where does the tour (go/start/finish)?	¿Dónde (va/empieza/termina) el tour?
What time does the tour (start/finish)?	¿A qué hora (empieza/termina) el tour?
Where do you buy tickets?	¿Dónde se compran los boletos?
How much does it cost?	¿Cuánto cuesta?
Are there any tickets for the concert?	¿Hay entradas para el concierto?
Do you need tickets?	¿Se necesitan boletos?

Va a . . .	It goes to . . .
Para en . . .	It stops at . . .
No se necesitan boletos.	You don't need tickets.
Es gratis.	It's free.
Perdone, están agotados.	Sorry, it's sold out.
En el Zócalo a las 8.	In the main square, at 8 o'clock.
Aquí puede comprarlos.	You can buy them here.
en la (taquilla/ventanilla)	in the ticket office
Está aquí (en el plano).	It's here (on the plan).

Getting in

Are there any tickets for (tonight/tomorrow)?	¿Hay boletos para (hoy en la noche/mañana)?
How much are they?	¿Cuánto cuestan?
Two (orchestra/balcony) tickets, please.	Dos boletos de (platea/anfiteatro), por favor.
How long does it last?	¿Cuánto dura?
Does it have subtitles?	¿Tiene subtítulos?
Is there an intermission?	¿Hay intermedio?
Is this seat (taken/free)?	¿Está (ocupado/libre) este asiento?
row	fila
orchestra seats	platea
balcony	anfiteatro
gallery	galería
cloakroom	guardarropa
(toilets for) (ladies/men)	(baño de) (damas/caballeros)
stairs	escalera
(emergency) exit	salida (de emergencia)
a program	un programa

Sport

Where can you play (tennis/golf)?	**¿Dónde se puede jugar al (tenis/golf)?**
Can I rent (a racket/a windsurf board?)	**¿Se puede alquilar (una raqueta/una tabla de wind-surf)?**
Where are the (locker rooms/the showers)?	**¿Dónde están (los vestidores/las regaderas)?**
fishing	**pescar**
horseback riding	**montar a caballo**
balls	**pelotas**
golf clubs	**palos de golf**
ping-pong table	**una mesa de ping pong**
tennis court	**una cancha de tenis**

On the beach

Where can you (sail/surf)?	**¿Dónde se puede (velear/hacer surfing)?**
diving	**bucear**
parasailing	**volar en paracaídas**
snorkeling	**bucear con esnórkel**
water skiing	**esquiar**
windsurfing	**hacer wind surf**
a (rowboat/motorboat)	**una lancha (de remos/de motor)**
chair	**una silla**
flippers	**aletas**
goggles	**gogles**
mask (with snorkel)	**un visor (con esnórkel)**
sailboat	**un velero**
sunshade	**una sombrilla**
table	**una mesa**
towel	**una toalla**
water skis	**esquis acuáticos**

ENTERTAINMENT AND LEISURE

Sound check

j is pronounced like the **ch** in "Loch Ness."

naranja	*nahrahnhha*
jugo	*hhoogoa*

Practice on these words:
**toronja   junto   lejos   jugar
oreja   jarabe   frijoles**

q is always followed by **u**, usually as **que** or **qui**. The **u** is then silent.

aquí	*ahkee*
qué	*keh*

Practice on these words:
**pulque   quinto   queso
boquerones   quince**

Language works

Getting to know the place

1 In the Tourist Office you find out there are mummies in Mexico
- ¿Qué hay que ver en aquí en Guanajuato?
- En las calles empedradas hay el Museo Casa Diego Rivera y el Museo de las Momias.
- ¿Momias?
- Sí. El Museo está aquí en el plano.
- Gracias.

(**momias** = mummies)

There are cobbled streets: true/false?
The mummies are in a museum: true/false?

Getting more information

2 You have heard that Machu Picchu is magical, so you ask about tours in your Cuzco hotel
- ¿Cuándo hay tours a Machu Picchu?
- Hay uno todos los días, a las siete de la mañana.
- ¿Dónde empieza?
- En la Plaza de Armas, y termina a las siete de la noche.
- ¿Dónde se compran los boletos?
- Aquí puede comprarlos.

How often are there tours to Machu Picchu?
How long does a tour last?

3 You ask for information at the hotel reception
- Me gusta la salsa. ¿Puede recomendarme una discoteca?
- Cómo no. El Madeiras.
- Y ¿a qué hora empieza?
- A las diez.

What time does the disco start?

On the beach

4 You have had enough of sitting on the beach and decide to go snorkeling
- ¿Se puede alquilar un visor?
- Sí, claro. ¿Quiere el visor solo o con aletas?
- ¿Cuánto cuesta con aletas?
- Cuarenta pesos la hora.
- Bien, deme un visor y unas aletas grandes.

How much will it cost to rent a mask and flippers for an hour?

Going to the Folklore Ballet

5 You are at the ticket office
- Dos boletos de platea para el martes, por favor.
- ¿Están bien estos en la fila F?
- Sí, están bien. ¿Cuánto dura el ballet?
- Dos horas y media.
- ¿Hay intermedio?
- Sí, veinte minutos.

How long does the show actually last?

Try it out

Leisure time

Unscramble the syllables to find out the things you can enjoy in Puerto Vallarta, México.
quiares tedralca
llesca drapedasem yapla
osepa en cobar carpes
rridasco de rosto
larvo en cadasírapa
tarmon a llocaba
cearbu con kelnóres

As if you were there

You ask for information on boat trips
- (Ask if there are boat trips)
- Sí, todos los días, a la Playa de Las Animas y a la Cascada de Quimixto.
- (Ask what time it leaves for the waterfall)
- A las nueve y media. Para cuarenta y cinco minutos en Los Arcos para bucear, y la comida es en Quimixto.
- (Ask if lunch is included)
- Sí, y hay barra libre en el barco.
- (Ask how much it costs)
- Cuarenta dólares.

Emergencies

Sources of information

Tourist information in Mexico is of uneven quality. In big cities, there are some helpful, well-stocked visitor bureaus that will give full details of local events. Elsewhere, though, you cannot expect much helpful guidance besides suggestions of places to stay and perhaps public transportation schedules.

Good sources of information are the English-language newspapers *The News* and *Mexico City Times*, both published in the capital and widely available elsewhere. The growth of cable and satellite TV services means that many hotels offer guests a number of US television networks, and in some you may also be able to receive BBC World TV.

Crime and safety

Mexico is a relatively safe destination, though as with any country there is a small minority of people who prey upon foreign tourists. Particular care should be taken on public transportation and at bus stations and airports. There is continuing political tension in the state of Chiapas. Travelers to this area should seek local advice.

! My wallet has been stolen.
Me robaron la cartera.

Emergency services

Some visitors who fall victim to petty crime comment that the police show little interest beyond providing an official record for insurance purposes. When driving, take particular care to obey regulations; many foreign motorists are stopped and obliged to pay heavy on-the-spot fines.

Every traveler to Mexico should arrange adequate insurance coverage with a company that offers a 24-hour medical emergency contact line. In the case of a serious medical complaint, or in the event of an accident, call this number if it is feasible; the duty doctors are trained to make quick, accurate decisions, and have contacts around the world who they can call on. Their involvement also means you should not be asked for payment or proof of resources before treatment. If time is critical, you can call an ambulance by dialing the number listed on the first or second page of the directory.

! I need an ambulance.
Necesito una ambulancia.

The standards of medical care have risen considerably, and in the larger cities hospitals match those found in other countries. However,

EMERGENCIES

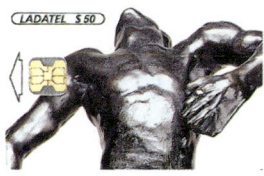

phone cards

for minor ailments, the best plan is to consult a local pharmacy (*farmacia*). These are easy to find in any town, and it is usually possible to find a pharmacist who speaks reasonable English. A wider range of medicines is available over the counter in Mexico than in many other countries. Keep receipts if you intend to make an insurance claim.

Staying healthy

Hygiene is normally good throughout Mexico, though visitors frequently encounter other problems. Stomach complaints are often the result of a change in diet rather than contamination, though hotel buffets – where food is left out in warm temperatures – can often be a source of unwelcome germs. A simple regime of rice with plain tea or coffee is a good antidote.

Most tap water is palatable, but mineral water is sold everywhere.

The high altitude in much of Mexico can cause respiratory difficulties, and in extreme cases lead to Altitude Sickness. Refrain from strenuous exertion and avoid alcohol.

A more common problem, particularly in the capital, is poor air quality; the English-language press publishes daily forecasts of the levels of toxins in the capital district.

Given that much of Mexico is within the Tropics, heat and sun can present dangers. In particular, avoid spending prolonged periods in the sun during the middle of the day.

Insects are more likely to be a nuisance rather than a danger, though in low-lying remote areas there is some risk of malaria. Consult your doctor shortly before departure.

Communications

The public telephone network is usually efficient, though there is a wide variety of types of phones and payment systems. You can make calls using coins, pre-paid cards (*tarjetas telefónicas*), credit cards or – possibly easiest of all – the home-country direct system, where you dial a number that connects you through to an operator in your country of residence.

Most hotels and other establishments have fax machines, which can facilitate making

99

reservations. Internet cafés, where you can rent a terminal and send e-mails, are just springing up in the larger cities.

The *oficina de correos* (post office) is at the center of every town. Mail services, however, are less than perfect, and you can expect the time taken by postcards to reach addresses abroad to be measured in weeks rather than days.

Electricity

The supply is 110 volts at 60 cycles per second, the same as in the US and Canada. The wide variety of sockets means that a travel adaptor is a good idea if you plan to use appliances. Note that this will not convert the supply for 240 volt appliances – a separate transformer is required.

Travelers with special needs

Mexico is not the ideal destination for disabled visitors. The need for ease of access has not yet been properly addressed in many places, and the average city walk constitutes a serious challenge for fully fit travelers because of the number and range of impediments.

Useful numbers

There is no fixed number for the emergency services; instead, each locality has its own, published on the first page or two of the telephone directory and in the local press.

Embassies in Mexico City

The number should be preceded by the dialing code 05 when dialing from other areas of Mexico, or +52 5 from outside the country.

United States: Paseo de la Reforma 305, Cuauhtémoc (208 4178).
Canada: Calle Schiller 529, Polanco (724 7900).
Australia: 10th floor, Plaza Polanco Torre B, Los Morales (254 4418).
Great Britain: Calle Río Lerma 71, Cuauhtémoc (207 2449).
New Zealand: 10th floor, Lagrange 103, Los Morales (281 5486).
South Africa: Andrés Bello 10, Forum Building, Polanco (282 9260).

Phrasemaker

Getting help and thanking people

Help!	¡Socorro!
Watch out!	¡Cuidado!
Hello there!	¡Oiga!
Excuse me!	¡Perdón!
Can you help me?	¿Me puede ayudar?
Where is the nearest (police station/garage/hospital)?	¿Dónde está (la delegación de policía más cercana/el taller más cercano/el hospital más cercano)?
I need (a doctor/an ambulance).	Necesito (un doctor/una ambulancia).
It's an emergency.	Es una emergencia.
Quickly!	¡Rápido!
Fire!	¡Fuego!
It's an earthquake.	Está temblando.
Do you speak English?	¿Habla usted inglés?
Thank you (very much).	(Muchas) gracias.
Leave me alone!	¡Déjeme en paz!
I'll call the police!	¡Voy a llamar a la policía!
Thief!	¡Ladrón!

Talking to a doctor or dentist

a doctor	un(a) doctor(a)
a dentist	un(a) dentista
I have a (very) sore . . . / I have a (bad) . . . ache.	Me duele (mucho) . . .
toothache (back teeth)	una muela
toothache (front teeth)	un diente
My . . . hurt (a lot).	Me duelen (mucho) . . .
It hurts here.	Me duele aquí.
It hurts a little.	Me duele un poco.
My (son/daughter) has an earache.	A mi (hija/hijo) le duele el oído.
My (wife's/husband's) kidneys hurt.	A mi (esposa/esposo) le duelen los riñones.

Parts of the body

ankle	**el tobillo**	chin	**la barba***
arm	**el brazo**	(inner) ear	**el oído**
back	**la espalda**	(outer) ear	**la oreja**
cheek	**la mejilla**	elbow	**el codo**
chest	**el pecho**	eyes	**los ojos**

EMERGENCIES

feet	**los pies**	liver	**el hídago**
fingers	**los dedos (de la mano)**	mouth	**la boca**
foot	**el pie**	neck	**el cuello**
forehead	**la frente**	nose	**la nariz**
hair	**el pelo**	shoulder	**el hombro**
hand	**la mano**	stomach	**el estómago**
head	**la cabeza**	thigh	**el muslo**
hip	**la cadera**	throat	**la garganta**
kidneys	**los riñones**	toes	**los dedos del pie**
knee	**la rodilla**	wrist	**la muñeca**
leg	**la pierna**		

* Argentina **la pera**

Other symptoms

I can't move my (arm).	**No puedo mover (el brazo).**
I'm allergic to (penicillin/antibiotics).	**Soy alérgico/a* (a la penicilina/a los antibióticos).**
I'm constipated.	**Estoy estreñido/a.**
I'm a diabetic.	**Soy diabético/a.**
I'm pregnant.	**Estoy en estado.**
I've vomited.	**Vomité.**
I've cut my finger.	**Me corté el dedo.**
I've burnt myself.	**Me quemé.**
A dog bit (me/him/her).	**(Me/Lo/La) mordió un perro.**
I've got . . .	**Tengo . . .**
My (son/daughter) has . . .	**Mi (hijo/hija) tiene . . .**
a broken (leg/arm)	**(el brazo roto/la pierna rota)**
stomach cramps	**retortijones**
a fever/asthma	**calentura/asma**
I feel (nauseated/chilled).	**Tengo (náuseas/escalofríos).**
I had a heart attack (a year/six months) ago.	**Tuve un infarto hace (un año/seis meses).**
I've got (high/low) blood pressure.	**Tengo la presión (alta/baja).**

* The **o** ending is for males, the **a** ending is for females

Necesito (examinarlo/examinarla).	I need to examine you.
No es nada grave.	It's nothing serious.
Tiene (gripe/una intoxicación/una infección).	You have (the flu/food poisoning/an infection).
¿Está vacunado contra (el tétano)?	Have you been vaccinated against (tetanus)?
el cólera	cholera
la tifoidea	typhoid
el paludismo	malaria
la hepatitis	hepatitis

EMERGENCIES

Tiene un hueso roto.	You have a broken bone.
Lo voy a enyesar.	I'm going to put it in a cast.
Hay que operar.	You need an operation.
Voy a (taparle/sacarle) la muela.	I'm going to (fill/extract) the tooth.
Dele . . .	Give (him/her) . . .
¿Le duele mucho?	Does it hurt a lot?
Tome (esta medicina/este remedio).	Take this medicine.
una cucharadita	one teaspoonful
Tome (estos antibióticos/estas pastillas).	Take these (antibiotics/pills).
Póngase esta (pomada/crema).	Put on this cream.
Póngase estas inyecciones.	Have these injections.
en seguida	right away
una vez al día	once a day
(dos/tres) veces al día	(twice/three times) a day
cada (cuatro) horas	every (four) hours
(antes/después) de las comidas	(before/after) meals
Tome mucha agua.	Drink lots of water.
No se ponga al sol.	Stay out of the sun.
Debe (descansar/dormir).	You must (rest/sleep).
No debe (levantarse/salir).	You mustn't (get up/go out).
Le voy a recetar . . .	I'm going to prescribe . . .
un analgésico	a painkiller
unas gotas	some drops
unas inyecciones	some injections
un jarabe	a syrup
una pomada	some cream
unas pastillas	some pills

Paying the fees

How much do I owe you?	¿Cuánto le debo?
May I have a receipt for my insurance?	¿Me puede dar un recibo para el seguro?

At the pharmacy

the pharmacy	la farmacia
the pharmacist	el/la farmacéutico/a
Do you have anything for . . . ?	¿Tiene algo para . . . ?
bites	las picaduras
constipation	el estreñimiento
a cough	la tos
diarrhea	la diarrea
a headache	el dolor de cabeza

EMERGENCIES

a rash	**el salpullido**
sunburn	**las quemaduras de sol**
sunstroke	**la insolación**
an upset stomach	**el malestar estomacal**
Do you have . . . ?	**¿Tiene . . . ?**
adhesive bandages	**curitas**
aspirin	**aspirina**
cough syrup	**jarabe para la tos**
a laxative	**un laxante**

Car breakdown

I've broken down.	**Se me descompuso el coche.**
The car has a flat tire.	**Se me ponchó una llanta.***
The (engine) isn't working.	**El (motor) no sirve.**
the accelerator	**el acelerador**
the brake	**el freno**
the clutch	**el clutch**
the radiator	**el radiador**
the steering wheel	**el volante**
The windshield wipers aren't working.	**Los limpiadores no sirven.**
the windows	**las ventanas**
the locks	**los seguros**
The car won't start.	**El coche no arranca.**
The battery is dead.	**La batería está baja.**
The lights aren't working.	**Las luces no encienden.**
Where is there a mechanic?	**¿Dónde hay un mecánico?**
I'm on the highway to Querétaro.	**Estoy en la autopista a Querétaro.**
I'm on the road to Cuzco.	**Estoy en la carretera a Cuzco.**
I'm (15) kilometers from Cuernavaca.	**Estoy a (quince) kilómetros de Cuernavaca.**
at kilometer 110	**en el kilómetro ciento diez**
Can you help me?	**¿Me puede ayudar?**
Do you have spare parts?	**¿Tiene refacciones?**
How long will it take?	**¿Cuánto tomará?**
When will it be ready?	**¿Cuándo estará listo?**
* Argentina	**Se me pinchó una rueda.**

¿Qué le pasa?	What's the matter?
¿Cuál es su (número de placa/ nombre)?	What's your (license plate number/name)?
ahorita/en seguida	right away
en dos horas	in two hours
Espere a Los Angeles Verdes.	Wait for The Green Angels (radio-equipped green repair trucks patrolling major Mexican highways. See p38)

Lost or stolen

I've lost my (wallet/passport).	**Perdí (la cartera/ el pasaporte).**
I've had my . . . stolen.	**Me robaron . . .**
briefcase	**el portafolio**
car	**el coche**
driver's license	**la licencia de manejar**
handbag	**la bolsa**
jewelry	**unas joyas**
money	**el dinero**
necklace	**un collar**
passport	**el pasaporte**
purse	**el monedero**
ring	**un anillo**
suitcase	**la maleta**
tickets	**los boletos**
wallet	**la cartera**

(five minutes/one hour) ago	**hace (cinco minutos/una hora)**
this morning	**hoy en la mañana**
yesterday (morning/afternoon)	**ayer en la (mañana/tarde)**
in (the street/a shop)	**en (la calle/una tienda)**
They took it from my bag.	**Me lo/la sacaron de la bolsa.**
I think	**Creo**
I don't know.	**No sé.**

¿Cuándo (fue el robo)?	When (was the robbery)?
¿Dónde?	Where?
¿Qué (traía en la bolsa)?	What (did you have in your bag)?
¿Cómo era?	What was it like?
¿Nombre?	Name?
Su pasaporte, por favor.	Your passport, please.
¿Sabe su número de pasaporte?	Do you know your passport number?
Llene esta forma.	Fill out this form.
Vuelva mañana.	Come back tomorrow.

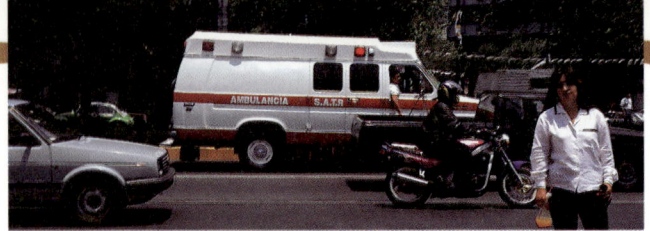

Sound check

r is pronounced in two ways, depending on its position in the word
■ With a single tap of the tongue just behind the front upper teeth.

doctor	*doaktoar*
aspirina	*ahspeereenah*

■ In initial position, strongly rolled

receta	*rehsehtah*
rápido	*rahpeedoah*

rr is always strongly rolled

carro	*kahrroa*
perro	*pehrroa*

Practice on these words:
**radiador   cadera   garganta
recibo   farmacia   socorro**

Language works

At the doctor

1 You ask about a stomach problem
■ **Me duele el estómago.**
□ **¿Está estreñida?**
■ **No, tengo diarrea.**
□ **Le voy a recetar unas pastillas. Tómelas cada ocho horas. Y tome mucha agua.**

What does the doctor prescribe?
What else should you do?

2 Your daughter is not well and you call the hotel doctor
■ **A mi hija le duele mucho un oído.**
□ **Le voy a recetar unas gotas, cada cuatro horas. Y dele una aspirina.**
■ **Muy bien, gracias.**

What did the doctor prescribe?

Getting help from the pharmacist

3 Sunburn strikes
■ **¿Tiene algo para las quemaduras de sol?**
□ **¿Le duele mucho?**
■ **Sí, los hombros y la espalda.**
□ **Póngase esta crema tres veces al día. Y no se ponga al sol.**
■ **Gracias. ¿Cuánto le debo?**

What do you have to do?

Transportation problems

4 You walk into a garage to report a breakdown.
□ **Buenos días. Se me descompuso el coche.**
■ **¿Qué le pasa?**
□ **No arranca.**
■ **¿Dónde está?**
□ **En la carretera a Tajín. Kilómetro sesenta y cinco. ¿Me puede ayudar?**
■ **Sí, pero hasta en la tarde.**
(**hasta** = not until)

How soon can you get help?

EMERGENCIES

I've been robbed!

5 You walk into a police station to report a robbery
- ■ ¡Me robaron la bolsa!
- □ ¿Cuándo fue el robo?
- ■ Hace media hora, en el metro.
- □ ¿Qué traía en la bolsa?
- ■ Mis cheques de viajero, dinero y mi pasaporte.
- □ ¿Sabe su número de pasaporte?
- ■ No, no sé.

What did the police officer want to know first?
What number did he ask about?

Try it out

Coyolxauhqui

In Aztec mythology, Coyolxauhqui, the sister of Huitzilopochtli, God of War, was thrown down the steps of a pyramid to punish her for trying to kill their mother. This stone representation of her dismembered body can be seen at the National Anthropology Museum in Mexico City. How many parts of her body can you identify?

Health concerns

Match the possible diagnosis with the symptoms described to the doctor and likely prescription. Each symptom might be characteristic of more than one illness, and each of the complaints might have more than one symptom.

POSIBLE DIAGNÓSTICO
infección
insolación
gripe

SÍNTOMA
diarrea
dolor de cabeza
escalofríos
calentura
náuseas
retortijones

RECETA
analgésico
antibiótico
pastillas
crema
jarabe

As if you were there

Your car won't start. You ask for help at the hotel reception desk
- ■ (Explain the problem and ask if they can help you)
- □ ¿Qué le pasa?
- ■ (You think the battery's dead. The lights don't work)
- □ Ahorita va el botones. ¿Cuál es su número de placa?

Language Builder
Gender

All Spanish nouns (words for things or people) are either masculine or feminine. A word's gender affects:
– the form of "a" and "the" used before it
– any adjectives (describing words) used with it

Most nouns ending in -**o** are masculine: **mercado**, **sombrero**. Most nouns ending in -**a** are feminine: **farmacia**, **casa**.

Words ending in other letters can be either masculine or feminine: you just have to learn them as you go along: **tomate** and **hotel** are masculine; **miel** and **calle** are feminine.

The articles: "a/an" and "the"
Remembering the gender of a word is easier if you memorize the word with an article.

	Masculine	Feminine
the	**el tomate** the tomato	**la miel** the honey
a	**un hotel** a hotel	**una calle** a street

Most names of occupations have a masculine and a feminine form: an -**a** replaces the masculine -**o** or is added at the end to form the feminine.

Masculine	Feminine
un secretario a male secretary	**una secretaria** a female secretary
el doctor the male doctor	**la doctora** the female doctor

But some stay the same; in these cases the gender of the person is shown by the article.

Masculine	Feminine
el dentista the male dentist	**la dentista** the female dentist
un estudiante a male student	**una estudiante** a female student

Singular and plural
To talk about more than one thing, add -**s** to a vowel ending and -**es** to a consonant ending.

Singular	Plural
libro book	**libros** books
catedral cathedral	**catedrales** cathedrals

The articles also have a plural form.

the	
Masculine	**los pollos** the chickens
Feminine	**las fresas** the strawberries

a/some Plural	
Masculine	**unos limones** some lemons
Feminine	**unas naranjas** some oranges

first floor

Adjectives

Most adjectives (describing words) have a masculine and a feminine form:
– an **-a** replaces the masculine **-o** or is added after the final consonant in adjectives of nationality.

Masculine	Feminine
el coche caro the expensive car	**la falda barata** the cheap skirt
un bar francés a French bar	**una uva inglesa** an English grape

but adjectives ending in **-a**, **-e** or a consonant (in adjectives of color) stay the same.

Masculine	Feminine
un templo azteca an Aztec temple	**una ciudad azteca** an Aztec city
el saco verde the green jacket	**la blusa verde** the green blouse
un vestido azul a blue dress	**una camisa azul** a blue shirt

Adjectives also have a singular and a plural form. As for nouns, you form the plural by adding **-s** to a vowel ending and **-es** to a consonant ending.

Singular	Plural
un saco rojo a red jacket	**dos sacos rojos** two red jackets
la flor azul the blue flower	**tres flores azules** three blue flowers

As you can see, in Spanish adjectives tend to go after the words they describe: **un muchacho alto** (a tall boy).

Verbs

In Spanish, you need to use a different verb form depending on whether you are addressing someone formally or informally. Here are different ways you would ask "How are you?" in Latin American Spanish:
¿Cómo está?
To an adult you have not met before or know only a little.
¿Cómo estás?
To a child or to an adult you are friendly with.
¿Cómo están?
To more than one person, whether you have just met them or are friendly with them

Verbs in Spanish change according to the person or thing they relate to (the subject), eg:
¿Cuánto cuesta el melón? (How much does the melon cost?)
¿Cuánto cuestan los melones? (How much do the melons cost?)
Tengo tos. (I have a cough.)
Mi hija tiene tos. (My daughter has a cough.)

Here is the full present tense of some useful irregular verbs:
tener (to have) and **ir** (to go).

tener	to have
tengo	I have
tienes	you (informal) have
tiene	you (formal) have
tiene	it/he/she has
tenemos	we have
tienen	you (plural formal and informal) have
tienen	they have

LANGUAGE BUILDER

ir	to go
voy	I go
vas	you (informal) go
va	you (formal) go
va	it/he/she goes
vamos	we go
van	you (plural formal and informal) go
van	they go

to be
There are two verbs meaning "to be" in Spanish:
ser is used to talk in general, about a permanent state;
estar is used for location (even if it is permanent) and for specific and temporary states.

Soy inglés.
I am English.
Estoy en Perú.
I am in Peru (now, I may leave tomorrow).
El caviar es caro.
Caviar is expensive (usually).
El sombrero está caro.
The hat is expensive (the one I saw).
Los aguacates mexicanos son buenos.
Mexican avocados are good (in general).
Los huevos estrellados están muy buenos.
The fried eggs are very good (the ones I am having or I've just had).

	ser	estar
I am	soy	estoy
you are (inf)	eres	estás
you are (formal)	es	está
it/he/she is	es	está
we are	somos	estamos
you are (plural)	son	están
they are	son	están

Questions

There are two ways to ask a question:
– turn the statement round
El banco está abierto.
The bank is open.
¿Está abierto el banco?
Is the bank open?
– use the same form as for the statement, but with a question intonation (tone going up).
¿El banco está abierto?
Is the bank open?

Things you like

To talk about what you like and dislike, you need the phrases **me gusta** and **me gustan**.

Me gusta el ajo, no me gusta la cebolla.
I like garlic, I don't like onion.
Me gustan las fresas, no me gustan los plátanos.
I like strawberries, I don't like bananas.

What the Spanish actually says is "Garlic is pleasing to me" and "Bananas aren't pleasing to me." So when you are talking about one thing, you use the singular **me gusta** and when you are talking about more than one, you use the plural **me gustan**.
Also note that you need to put in **el**, **la**, **los** or **las** before the thing(s) you (don't) like.
Me gusta el tequila.
No me gustan los hongos.

LANGUAGE BUILDER

Talking about possession

The word **de** is used before the name of the owner
El libro de Juan Juan's book

To talk about "my book," "his car" etc., use these forms. They are singular or plural, to agree with the item or items possessed.
su libro her book
sus maletas her suitcases

mi	mis	my
tu	tus	your (informal)
su	sus	your (formal)
su	sus	his/her
nuestro/a nuestros/as*		our
su	sus	your (plural formal & informal)
su	sus	their

*"our" has a masculine and a feminine form, according to the gender of the items possessed (not the gender of the owners).
nuestro hotel our hotel
nuestras hijas our daughters

This, that, these, those (ones)

These words are adjectives, so they agree with the noun in gender and in number.

este libro/estos libros
this book/these books
esta revista/estas revistas
this magazine/these magazines
ese libro/esos libros
that book/those books
esa revista/esas revistas
that magazine/those magazines

These words can also be used like pronouns (eg "this one") when it is clear what they refer to.

¿Cuánto cuesta éste?
How much is this one?
Note that in these cases, they take an accent.

Very, very much/many and a lot (of)

– **muy** before an adjective means "very."
El tequila está muy bueno.
The tequila is very good.
– **mucho** after a verb means "very much" or "a lot."
Me gusta mucho esta salsa.
I like this salsa a lot.
– **mucho** before a noun means "many/much/a lot of." But in this case it changes with the number and gender of the noun.
No bebo mucho vino.
I don't drink much wine.
Tomar mucha agua.
You drink a lot of water.
Hay muchos bares.
There are many bars.

it, them

Pronouns in Spanish change depending on the gender and number of the noun they replace.
el suéter – ¿Puedo probármelo?
Can I try it on? (masculine singular)
la camisa – ¿Puedo probármela?
Can I try it on? (feminine singular)
los jeans – Me los llevo.
I'll take them. (masculine plural)
las medias – Me las llevo.
I'll take them. (feminine plural)

Answers

Bare necessities
1 13 pesos 2 about 800 pesos; passport 3 Have a good day.

Missing vowels
cuatro; ocho; diez; dieciséis; veinte; cincuenta; noventa; cien; trescientos; mil

Get it right
1 ¿Dónde está el baño?
2 Buenas noches.
3 ¡Salud!
4 Con permiso, por favor.
5 ¿Cuánto cuestan los aretes?
6 ¿Hay elevador?/¿Dónde está el elevador?
7 ¡Perdón!

As if you were there
- Más despacio, por favor.
- Sí.
- Soy [nationality], de [home town].
- ¿Cómo?
- Mucho gusto Sr Parra. Me llamo [your name].

Getting around
1 no, two blocks away 2 2,000 pesos 3 check the oil 4 true 5 line 2, direction Tasqueña 6 every hour; six hours

Find the right place
1 el Correo 2 una tienda de artesanías 3 la terminal de autobuses 4 una farmacia 5 la Oficina de Turismo 6 la alberca 7 una gasolinería

Mix and match
1 e 2 d 3 b 4 a 5 c

As if you were there
- ¿Pasa por Bellas Artes?
- ¿Cuánto es a Bellas Artes?
- Aquí tiene. ¿Me dice dónde bajarme?
- Gracias.

Somewhere to stay
1 400 pesos 2 true; false 3 700 pesos; show your passport and fill out a form 4 true; true 5 yes

"A" puzzle
1 habitación 2 llave 3 elevador 4 restaurante 5 desayuno

As if you were there
- No hay papel de baño.
- Gracias. ¿Me puede despertar a las siete, por favor?

Buying things
1 by ten pesos 2 because there weren't any; 24 pesos 3 red and blue 4 a Mexican newspaper in English 5 tomorrow afternoon

Food mixer
jugo; plátano; jamón; sandía; alcachofa; queso; huevo; naranja; leche; lechuga

Phrase matcher
1 c 2 e 3 a 4 b 5 d

As if you were there
- Es muy bonita. ¿De qué está hecha?
- ¿Cuánto cuesta?
- ¿Se aceptan tarjetas de crédito?
- ¿Es el último precio?
- Me la llevo./Gracias, es muy cara.

Café life
1 chicken, ham, beefsteak
2 if you want beefsteak or pork chops, and which soft drink you want 3 because they had no Corona 4 false; true 5 gin

ANSWERS

Crossword
1 pistache; 2 mango; 3 melón;
4 fresa; 5 elote
Mystery drink: chocolate

Split the difference
tequila; descafeinado; refresco; limonada; cacahuate; jugo; churro; sangría; cerveza; margarita
cacahuate and *churro* are not drinks

As if you were there
- Buenas tardes. Un té negro con leche. ¿Qué refrescos tiene?
- Coca/Sprite/Una malteada, por favor.
- Y dos buñuelos.
- Unos churros.

Eating out
1 true 2 fish stewed in the oven with tomatoes, onion, peppers and olives 3 yes; no 4 pineapple, watermelon and melon

As if you were there
- Buenos días. Una mesa para dos, afuera, por favor.
- Dos jugos de naranja, huevos con jamón y waffles con miel de maple.
- Dos jarras de café . . . y un tenedor.

Entertainment and leisure
1 true; true 2 every day; twelve hours 3 at 10 pm 4 40 pesos 5 two hours and ten minutes

Leisure time
esquiar; catedral; calles empedradas; playa; paseo en barco; pescar; corridas de toros; volar en paracaídas; montar a caballo; bucear con esnórkel

As if you were there
- ¿Hay paseos en barco?
- ¿A qué hora sale a Quimixto?
- ¿Está incuida la comida?
- ¿Cuánto cuesta?

Emergencies
1 some pills; drink a lot of water 2 some drops every four hours and an aspirin 3 apply the cream three times a day and stay out of the sun 4 not until the afternoon 5 when the robbery had taken place; passport number

Coyolxauhqui

Health concerns
Infección: diarrea, retortijones, náuseas, dolor de cabeza; jarabe, pastillas, antibiótico
Insolación: dolor de cabeza, escalofríos, náuseas, calentura; pastillas, analgésico
Gripe: dolor de cabeza, tos; analgésico, jarabe (para la tos)

As if you were there
- Mi coche no arranca. ¿Me puede ayudar?
- La batería está baja. Las luces no encienden.

Dictionary

a fines de at the end of
a la carta à la carte
a mano derecha on the right
a mano izquierda on the left
abierto/a open
abrigo, el coat
abrir to open
aceite, el oil
aceituna, la olive
acelerador, el accelerator
adentro inside
adiós goodbye
adulto/a adult
aeropuerto, el airport
afuera outside
agua, el (f) water
agua de jamaica, el (f) water flavored with hibiscus
agua mineral con gas/sin gas, el (f) carbonated/noncarbonated mineral water
aguacate, el avocado
ahora now
aire acondicionado/a air conditioned
ajedrez, el chess
ajo, el garlic
al horno cooked in the oven
albahaca, la basil
alberca, la swimming pool
alcachofa, la artichoke
alcoba, la berth
alérgico/a allergic
aletas, las flippers
algo something, rather
algodón, el cotton
almohada, la pillow
alquilar to rent
amarillo/a yellow
ambulancia, la ambulance
analgésico, el painkiller
ananá, la pineapple
andén, el platform
anfiteatro, el balcony
anillo, el ring
año, el year
anoche last night
antes before

antibióticos, los antibiotics
antiguo/a former, old
apartamento, un apartment
aparte separate
apio, el celery
aretes, los earrings
arrancar el coche to start the car
arte, el art
artesanía, la craftsmanship
asiento, un seat
asma, el asthma
aspirina, la aspirin
autobús, el bus
autopista, la highway
avión, el airplane
ayer yesterday
ayer en la mañana/tarde yesterday morning/afternoon
ayudar to help
azúcar, el sugar
azul blue

bahía, la bay
bajarse del metro/autobús to get off the train/bus
bajo/a low/short
ballet, el ballet
banana, la banana
banco, el bank
baño, el restroom, bathroom
bar, el bar
barato/a cheap
barba, la chin
barquillo, un cone
barro, el earthenware, mud
bastante quite, rather
basurero, el trash can
batería, la car battery
beber to drink
bebida fría/caliente, una cold/hot drink
beige beige
berenjena, la eggplant
bicicleta, la bicycle
bici-taxi, el cycle rickshaw
bien good
bienvenido/a welcome
bistec, el beefsteak
blanco/a white
blusa, la blouse
boca, la mouth

DICTIONARY

boite, una nightclub (Argentina)
boleto, el ticket
boleto de ida/de ida y vuelta, el single/return ticket
bolsa, la bag
boquerones, los fresh anchovies
bordado/a embroidered
botas, las boots
botella, la bottle
botones, el bellboy
brasier, el bra
brazo, el arm
brecha, la track/path
brevete, el driver's license (Peru)
bucear to dive
¡buen provecho! enjoy your meal!
buenas noches good evening / night
buenas tardes good afternoon / evening
bueno OK
buenos días good morning
buzón, el mailbox

caballeros men
cabaña, la hut
cabeza, la head
cacahuetes, los peanuts
cada each, every
cadera, la hip
café brown
café, el coffee, café
café americano, el black coffee
café con crema, el black coffee with milk on the side
café con leche, el coffee with cream
café de olla, el black coffee with raw cane sugar and cinnamon
café descafeinado, el decaffeinated coffee
café espresso, el espresso coffee
café negro, el black coffee
cafetería, la café
caja, la box
caja fuerte, la safe-deposit box
caja permanente, la automatic teller machine
cajero automático, el automatic teller machine
calavera, la skull

calentura, la temperature, fever
caliente hot
calle, la street
calles empedradas, las cobbled streets
calzoncillos, los briefs
calzones, los boxer shorts
cama individual, la single bed
cama matrimonial, la double bed
cambiar to change
cambio, el change, exchange
camisa, la shirt
camiseta, la T-shirt
campera, la jacket (Argentina)
camping, un campsite
cancha de tenis, la tennis court
cantina, la (rough) bar
capuchino, el cappuccino
carnicería, la butcher
caro/a expensive
carretera, la road
carril, el road lane
carro, el car
carta, la menu
cartera, la wallet
casa, la house
casa de cambio, la bureau de change
casa de huéspedes, la guest house
cascada, la waterfall
caseta de cobro, la tollbooth
castillo, el castle
catedral, la cathedral
caviar, el caviar
cazuela, la cooking pot
cebolla, la onion
cena, la dinner
central de autobús, el bus station
centro, el town center
centro comercial, el shopping center
cerámica, la ceramics
cerca close
cerradura, la lock
cerrado/a closed
cerrar to close
cerveza, la beer
cerveza clara/oscura, la light/dark beer
chabacano, el apricot

DICTIONARY

chamarra de piel, la leather jacket
champaña, la champagne
champiñones, los mushrooms
charola, la tray
cheque de viajero, el traveler's check
chícharos, los peas
chico/a small
chico/a, el/la boy/girl
chile, el hot pepper
chocolate, el chocolate
chófer, un driver
chuleta, la pork chop
cine, el movie
cinturón, el belt
ciruela, la plum
ciudad, la city
¡claro! of course
clutch, el clutch
cobija, la blanket
cobre, el copper
coche, el car
coche de alquiler, el rental car
cocina, la stove/kitchen
coco, el coconut
codo, el elbow
col, la cabbage
cólera, el cholera
coliflor, la cauliflower
collar, el necklace
comer to eat
comida, la lunch
¿cómo? pardon?
¿cómo está? how are you?
comprar to buy
con with
coñac, el cognac
concierto, el concert
conducir to drive
conseguir to get, to manage
construcción, la construction
copa, la glass
corbata, la tie
Correo, el Post Office
corrida de toro, la bullfight
cortarse to cut yourself
costa, la coast
costilla, la rib of meat
creer to believe
crema, la cream, ointment
crudo/a raw
¿cuándo? when?
¿cuánto? how much?
¿cuánto cuesta(n)? how much does it/they cost?
cuarto, el room (Mexican)
cuarto (de kilo), el 250 grams
cuba, la rum and coke
cuchara, la spoon
cucharadita, la teaspoonful
cucharita, la teaspoon
cuchillo, el knife
cuello, el neck
cuenta, la bill
cuero, el leather
cuerpo, el body
cuesta, la hill, incline
¡cuidado! watch out!
cuota, la toll
curitas, las adhesive bandages
curva, la bend

Damas Ladies
de from, about
de nada you're welcome
¿de qué está hecho/a? what is it made of?
¿de verdad? really?
deber to owe
dedo, el finger
dedo del pie, el toe
dejar to leave
¡déjeme en paz! leave me alone!
delegación de policía, la police station
dentista, el/la dentist
depósito, el deposit
derecha, la right
desayuno, el breakfast
descansar to rest
descomponer to break down
desinfectado/a disinfected
despacio slowly
despertar to wake up
después after
día, el day
diabético/a diabetic
diapositivas, las photographic slides
diarrea, la diarrhea
dinero, el money

dirección, la direction
discoteca, la disco
doblado/a dubbed
docena, la dozen
doctor/a, el/la doctor
dólar, el US dollar ($)
doler to hurt
dolor de cabeza, el headache
¿dónde (está)...? where (is)...?
dormir to sleep
ducha, la shower
duele it hurts, it's sore
dulce sweet
durar to last
durazno, el peach

efectivo, el cash
ejotes, los green beans
elevador, el lift
elote, el sweet corn
embajada, la embassy
emergencia, la emergency
empezar to start, to begin
en estado pregnant
en las rocas on the rocks
encender to turn something on
enfrente opposite
ensalada, la salad
enseguida right away
entrada, la ticket (for concert/film)
enyesar to put in a plaster cast
error, el mistake
escalera, la staircase
escalofríos, los chills
escribir to write
esnórkel, el snorkel
espalda, la back
espárragos, los asparagus
especie, una a sort of
espectáculo, el entertainment event
esposa, la wife
esquiar to ski
esquina, la corner
esquís acuáticos, los water skis
estación, la train station
estacionamiento, el parking lot
estacionar to park
estampilla, la postage stamp
estar to be

estómago, el stomach
estreñido/a constipated
estreñimiento, el constipation
estufa, la stove
examinar to examine
excusado, el toilet; restroom
exhibición, la exhibition/showing
extranjero/a foreign

falda, la skirt
faltar to be lacking
farmacéutico/a, el/la pharmacist
farmacia, la pharmacy
faro, el lighthouse
feria, la fair
festival, el festival
fiesta, la fiesta
fila, la row, line
fin de semana, el weekend
final, el end
firma, la signature
firmar to sign
flor, la flower
folklor, el folklore
fonda, la reasonably priced restaurant
forma, la form, shape
frasco, el jar
frenar to brake
frenos, los brakes
frente, la forehead
fresa, la strawberry
frijoles, los kidney beans
frío/a cold
frutería, la fruit shop
¡fuego! fire!
fuegos artificiales, los fireworks
fumar to smoke
fumar/no fumar (no) smoking
funcionar to work/function
fútbol, el football

galería, la gallery
galería de arte, la art gallery
galleta, la cookie
gancho, el hanger
garbanzos, los chick peas
garganta, la throat
gasolina (sin plomo), la (unleaded) gasoline
gasolinera, la gas station

DICTIONARY

gerente, el/la manager
gogles, los goggles
golf, el golf
golfito, el miniature golf
gotas, las drops (medical)
gracias thank you
gramo, un gram
gran(de) big
grave serious
gripe, la flu
guagua, la bus (Caribbean)
guanábana, la soursop
guardarropa, el cloakroom
guayabera, la white cotton shirt-jacket
guía, el/la guide (person)
guía, la guide (book)
guitarra, la guitar

habitación, la room
habitación doble, la double room
habitación individual/sencillo, la single room
hablar to talk/speak
hace (dos horas) (two hours) ago
hacer to do/make
hacer surfing/wind surf to surf/wind surf
hacienda, una first-class hotel/restaurant
hamaca, la hammock
hamburguesa, la hamburger
hasta el lunes see you on Monday
hasta luego see you later
hasta mañana see you tomorrow
¿hay . . . ? is there/are there . . . ?
hay que . . . it is necessary to . . .
hecho/a a mano handmade
helado, el ice cream
hepatitis, la hepatitis
hígado, el liver
higo, el fig
hijo/a, el/la son/daughter
hojalata, la tinplate
¡hola! hello!
hombre, el man
Hombres Men
hombro, el shoulder
hongos, los mushrooms
hora, la hour, time
horario, el timetable

horongo, el poncho
hotel, el hotel
hoy today
hoy en la mañana this morning
hoy en la noche tonight
huaraches, los sandals
hueso, el bone
huevo, el egg
huipil, el overblouse

iglesia, la church
impuestos, los taxes
incluido/a included
infarto, el heart attack
infección, la infection
insolación, la sunstroke
interesarse to be interested in
intermedio, el intermission
intoxicación, la food poisoning
inyección, la injection
isla, la island
IVA, el sales tax
izquierda, la left

jabón, el soap
jamón, el ham
jarabe, el syrup, medicine
jarabe para la tos, el cough syrup
jardín, el garden
jarra, la jug
jarro, el earthenware jug
jeans, los jeans
jitomate, el tomato
joyas, las jewelry
joyería, la jeweler
juego, el game
jugar to play
jugo, el juice, liquidized fruit drink
junto a next to

kilo, un kilo
kilometraje, el mileage
kilómetro, un kilometer

ladrón, el thief
lago, el lake
lámpara, la lamp
lana, la wool
lancha de remos/motor, la row-/motor boat
laqueado/a lacquered

DICTIONARY

lata, la tin
latón, el brass
laxante, el laxative
le falta you/it need(s)
leche, la milk
lechuga, la lettuce
lejos far
levantarse to get up
libertad, la freedom
libra, la British pound (£)
libre free (unoccupied)
librería, la bookstore
libro, el book
licencia de manejar, la driver's license
licuado, el juice, liquidized fruit drink
limón, el lemon/lime
limpiadores, los windshield wipers
línea, la line (subway)
listo/a ready
litro, el liter
llamar to telephone/call
llamarse to be called
llanta, la tire
llave, la key
llave del agua, la faucet
llavero, el key ring
llegar to arrive
llenar (de) to fill (with)
lleno/a full
lleva (pollo) it's got (chicken) in it
llevar to carry, to take
lonchería, la simple fast-food restaurant
lugar, el place
lujo, el luxury
luz, la light

maceta, la flowerpot
madera, la wood
maestro/a, el/la teacher
mágico/a magic
maíz, el corn
malestar estomacal, el upset stomach
maleta, la suitcase
malteada, la drink made with milk and liquidized fruit/ice cream
mañana, la tomorrow, the morning

mandar to send
mango, el mango
mano, la hand
mantequilla, la butter
manzana, la apple
mapa, el map
maracuyá, el passion fruit
margarina, la margarine
marido, el husband
mariscos, los seafood
martini (seco), el (dry) martini
marzo March
mayo May
me duele ... my ... hurts
me llamo my name is
¿me puede ayudar? can you help me?
mecánico, el mechanic
media botella, la half a bottle
media docena half a dozen
mediados de, a in the middle of
medianoche midnight
medias, las stockings
medicina, la medicine
medio/a half
medio kilo half a kilo
mediodía midday
mejilla, la cheek
melón, el melon
menú del día, el menu of the day
mercado, el market
mesa, la table
mesa de ping pong, la ping-pong table
mesero/a, el/la waiter/waitress
mestizo/a mixed-race
metro, el subway
metro, un meter
miel, la honey
milanesa, la veal escalope
mimbre, el wicker
mirar to look at
miscelánea, la general store
mitad, la half
momia, la mummy
moneda, la coin
monedero, el purse
montaña, la mountain
montar a caballo to go riding
monte, el small mountain
monumento, el monument

DICTIONARY

morder to bite
motel, el motel
motor, el engine
mover to move
muchacho/a, el/la boy, girl
mucho/a a lot
muela, la molar
muerto/a dead
mujer, la woman, wife
Mujeres ladies
muñeca, la wrist
museo, el museum
música, la music
muslo, el thigh
muy very

nacional national
nada nothing
naranja, la orange
nariz, la nose
náusea, la nausea
Navidad, la Christmas
necesitar to need
negro/a black
nevería, la ice cream/sorbet shop
nieve, la sorbet/snow
nightclub, el nightclub
niño/a, el/la child
no no
no funciona it doesn't work
no importa it doesn't matter
noche, la night
nombre, el name
nos vemos see you later
nos vemos (mañana) see you (tomorrow)
nuevo/a new
nuez, la walnut
número, el number/shoe size
número de placa, el license plate

Oficina de Turismo, la tourist information office
oído, el (inner) ear
¡oiga! hey!/excuse me!
ojo, el eye
ópera, la opera
operador/a, el/la switchboard operator
operar to operate
orden, el order (tidiness)
orden, la order (command)
oreja, la (outer) ear
oro, el gold

pagar to pay
paja, la straw
palacio, el palace
paleta de..., una a...popsicle
palomitas, las popcorn
palos de golf, los golf clubs
paludismo, el malaria
pan, el bread
panadería, la bakery
pantalones, los pants
pantimedias, las tights
papa, la potato
papagayo, el parrot
papas fritas, las potato chips
papel, el paper
papel de baño, el toilet paper
papelería, la stationery store
papier mâché, el papier mâché
paquete, el packet
para llevar to carry out
para servirle you're welcome (at your service)
parada, la bus/train stop
parada de guaguas, la bus stop (Caribbean)
parque, el park
parroquia, la parish
partido de fútbol, el soccer match
pasado mañana the day after tomorrow
pasaporte, el passport
pasar por to go past/through
paseo, un stroll, walk
pastel, el cake
pastelería, la cake shop
pastillas, las pills
paté, el pâté
pecho, el chest
película, la film
peligroso/a dangerous
pelo, el hair
pelota, la ball
peluquería, la barber
pensar to think
pensarlo to think about it
pensión, la boardinghouse
pepino, el cucumber

DICTIONARY

pepitas, las pumpkin seeds
pera, la pear ("chin" in Argentina)
perder to lose
¡perdón! excuse me!
perdón/perdone sorry
perejil, el parsley
periódico, el newspaper
pero but
perro (caliente), el (hot) dog
persona, la person
pescado, el fish
pescar to go fishing
pesero, el privately owned minibus service
peso, el Mexican currency ($)
picadura, la insect bite
picar to be spicy/hot
pie, el foot
pierna, la leg/leg of pork
pila, la battery
pimiento, el pepper
piña, la pineapple
piña colada, la piña colada
pintado/a painted
pintura, la painting
pirámides, las pyramids
piscina, la swimming pool
piso, el floor (story)
pistache, el pistachio
pizza, la pizza
plano, el plan, map
planta baja, la ground floor
plata, la silver
plátano, el banana
platea, la stalls in theater
platito, el saucer
plato, el dish (food)
plato principal, el main course
playa, la beach
playera, la T-shirt
plaza de armas, la main square (Peru/Argentina)
plaza mayor, la main square (Central America/Caribbean)
poco, un a little
pollo, el chicken
pomada, la cream
ponchar una llanta to burst a tire
poncho, el poncho
poner to put (on)
¿por cuánto tiempo? for how long?

por favor please
por persona per person
poro, el leek
portafolio, el briefcase
posada, la small hotel
postre, el dessert
precio, el price
preferir to prefer
presidencia municipal, la town hall
presión, la blood pressure
principios de, a at the beginning of
programa, el program
¿puede . . . ? can/could you . . . ?
puedo I can
¿puedo probármelo(s)/la(s)? can I try it/them on?
puente, un bridge
puerta, la gate/door
puerto, el port
puesto, el a stall
puesto de periódicos, un newspaper stand
pulsera, la bracelet
purificado/a purified

¿qué? what?
¿qué le pasa? what's the matter?
quedar bien to suit, go with
quedarse to stay
quemaduras de sol, las sunburn
quemarse to burn yourself
queso, el cheese
quetzal, el Guatemalan currency
quisiera . . . I'd like . . .

rábano, el radish
radiador, el radiator
¡rápido! quickly!
raqueta, la racket
rebozo, el shawl
recamarera, la chambermaid
recomendar to recommend
recepcionista, el/la receptionist
recetar to prescribe
recibo, el receipt
refacciones, las spare parts
refresco (embotellado), el (bottled) soft drink
regadera, la shower
registro, el driver's license (Argentina)

DICTIONARY

remedio, el remedy, medicine
rentar to rent
reparación, la repair
repetir repeat
reservación, la reservation
reservar to reserve/book
restaurante, el restaurant
retortijones, los stomach cramps
revelar to reveal/to develop photos
revisar to check
revista, la magazine
rico/a rich
riesgo, el risk
riñon, el kidney
río, el river
robar to steal
robo, el theft
rodilla, la knee
rojo/a red
rollo a colores/en blanco y negro roll of color/black and white film
rollo de papel de baño, el roll of toilet paper
romper to break
rompope, el eggnog
ron, el rum
rosa pink
rosado, el (vino) rosé wine
roto/a broken
ruedas, las tires (Argentina)
ruinas, las ruins

saber to know
sacar to take out
sacarina, la artificial sweetener
saco, el jacket
sacrificio, el sacrifice
salida (de emergencia), la (emergency) exit
salir to leave, go out
salón de baile, el dance hall
salón de belleza, la beauty parlor/hairdresser
salpullido, el rash
¡salud! cheers!
sandalias, las sandals
sandía, la watermelon
sándwich, el sandwich
santo/a holy
santo/a, un(a) saint

seco dry
seda, la silk
seguro, el insurance
seguros, los locks
selva, la forest
semana, la week
semana que viene, la next week
semana pasada, la last week
señor/señora/señorita sir/madam/miss
septiembre September
ser to be
servibar, el minibar
servicio, el service/service charge
servicio de lavandería, el laundry service
servicio en el cuarto room service
servilleta, una napkin
shorts, los shorts
sí yes
sillla, la chair
sin without
sitio de taxis, un taxi stand
sobre, el envelope
¡socorro! help!
sol, el sun
sólo only
solo/a alone/neat
sombrerería, la hat shop
sombrero, el hat
sombrilla, la sunshade
sostén, el bra (Central America/Argentina)
soy I am
subte, el subway (Argentina)
subtítulos, los subtitles
suéter, el sweater
supermercado, el supermarket

tabla de wind-surf, la windsurf board
talla, la size (clothes)
tallado/a carved
taller, el workshop
tapete, el rug
taquería, la taco restaurant
taquilla, la ticket office
tarda x minutos it takes x minutes
tarde, la afternoon
tarjeta de crédito, la credit card

Sounds Spanish

Spanish pronunciation is very consistent. You can easily tell how a word is pronounced from the way it is written and there are very few silent letters.

Vowels

There are only five vowel sounds in Spanish.
- **a** like "a" in "father"
  casa
- **e** like "e" in "Ben"
  tele
- **i** like "ee" in "been"
  mira
- **o** like "o" in "nod"
  loco
- **u** like "oo" in "food"
  uno

(although in the combinations **gue**, **gui**, **que** and **qui** the **u** is silent, unless it is written **ü**)

The vowels represent the same sounds wherever they appear in a word.

Diphthongs

The combinations of two weak vowels (**i** and **u**) with each other or a weak vowel with a strong vowel (**a**, **e** and **o**) are run together in one syllable, but the vowels keep their original sound
¿C**ua**nto c**ue**sta?
V**ei**nte **au**strales.

Two strong vowels together count as two separate syllables.

Consonants

The consonants are pronounced as follows.

- **c** before "e" and "i," like "s" in "salt"
  cerca
  cinta
  otherwise like in "car"
  con
  claro
- **d** like "d" in "duck"
  dólar
- **f** like "f" in "fat"
  fresa
- **k** like "k" in "kick"
  (only in foreign words)
  kilo
- **l** like "l" in "lake"
  melón
- **m** like "m" in "mother"
  más
- **n** like "n" in "no"
  tren
- **p** like p in "pot"
  padre
- **s** like s in "sack"
  usted
- **t** like t in "teacher"
  filete
- **w** like w in "water"
  (only in foreign words)
  whisky

Listen to these a bit more carefully.
b and **v** at the beginning of a word and after "n" or "m," like "b" in "but"
  bueno
  cambio
  invierno
otherwise softer, more like "v" in "very"
  nuevo
  libra

DICTIONARY

tarjeta de turista, la official tourist card
tarjeta postal, la postcard
tarjeta telefónica, la phone card
tarro, el mug
taxi, el taxi
taxímetro, el taxi price meter
taza, la cup
té, el tea
té de manzanilla, el camomile infusion
té helado, el iced tea
teatro, el theater
tejido/a knitted
teléfono, el telephone
televisión, la television
templo, el religious temple
tenedor, el fork
tenemos we have
tenis, el tennis
tengo I have
tequila, la tequila
terminal, la bus station
terminar to finish
tétano, el tetanus
textil, el textile
tianguls, un market (Mexican)
tienda, la shop/tent
¿tiene . . . do you have . . . ?
tifoidea, la typhoid
timbre, el postage stamp
tinto, el vino red wine
tipo, el type
toalla, la towel
tobillo, el ankle
todo/a(s) all/everything/every
tomar to have (food)
tomate, el tomato
toronja, la grapefruit
torta, la sandwich roll
torre, la tower
tos, la cough
tour, el tour
trabajo, el work
traje de baño, el bathing suit
trailer, el camper
tren, el train
turquesa, la turquoise

último/a, el/la the last
uvas, las grapes

vacío/a empty
vacunado/a contra vaccinated against
vainilla, la vanilla
valle, el valley
vaso, el glass
vegetariano/a vegetarian
velear to sail
velero, el sailboat
velocidad, la speed
vender to sell
ventana, la window
ventanilla, la ticket office (Argentina)
ventilador, el fan
ver to see
verano, el summer
verdad, la truth
verdulería, la produce store
vermut, el vermouth
vestido, el dress
vestidores, los locker rooms
vez, la time
vez al día, una once a day
viaje, el journey/trip
vidrio (soplado), el (hand-blown) glass
viejo/a old
villa juvenil, la youth hostel
vino, el wine
visita, la visit
visor, el diving mask
vista al mar, una ocean view
vivir to live
vodka, el vodka
volante, el steering wheel
volar en paracaídas to parasail
volver to return
vomitar to be sick

water, el toilet
whisky, el whisky

yogurt, el yogurt

zanahoria, la carrot
zapatería, la shoe store
zapatos, los shoes
zócalo, el main square
zona, la area